PARTNERS IN HEALING

PARTNERS IN HEALING

*Bringing Compassion to People
with Illness or Loss—
A Handbook*

edited by
Beverly Anne Musgrave
and John R. Bickle

PAULIST PRESS
New York/Mahwah, N.J.

Book design by Celine M. Allen

Cover design by Valerie Petro

Library of Congress Cataloging-in-Publication Data

Partners in healing : bringing compassion to people
with illness or loss : a handbook / edited by Beverly Anne Musgrave
and John R. Bickle.
        p. cm.
Includes bibliographical references.
   ISBN 0-8091-4172-8
  1. Church work with the sick. 2. Church work with the bereaved.
  3. Visitation (Church work) I. Musgrave, Beverly Anne. II. Bickle, John.
   BV4460 .P34 2003
   259'.4—dc21

                                        2002156420

Published by Paulist Press
997 Macarthur Boulevard
Mahwah, New Jersey 07430

www.paulistpress.com

Printed and bound in the
United States of America

Contents

Introduction
Beverly Anne Musgrave vii

PART I: THE MEANING OF ILLNESS

The Spiritual Pain of Illness: Finding Meaning in Loss
John R. Bickle...3

The Spiritual Challenge of Illness: Hope
Elizabeth M. Renyi 15

PART II: ISSUES FOR VISITORS

Empathy: The Caregiver Looks Both Ways
Beverly Anne Musgrave...31

Visiting Those Who Mourn
Sarah L. Fogg 45

Presence: An Active Silence
Beverly Anne Musgrave...67

The Costly Business of Being a Care Partner
Beverly Anne Musgrave...84

A Healing Presence: Meetings with Patients
  Jacqueline C. Perez, D.O...101

Health Issues for Visitors
  Kathleen M. Duffy...115

Confidence and Confidentiality:
The Ethics of Pastoral Visitation
  Curtis W. Hart...127

PART III: SUPPORTING VISITATION PROGRAMS

Practical Steps to Developing Effective Volunteers
  Patricia Cusack, O.P....139

Common Ground:
The Importance of Group Support for Visitors
  Elizabeth A. Baker..146

Critical Issues in the Development
of a Pastoral Visitation Program
  Michelle D. White 162

Contributors to This Volume...179

Introduction

Beverly Anne Musgrave

When one comes to a place in life where time stands still and life is defined by waiting, waiting, waiting, you are either on retreat or in a doctor's office. Both situations are different and similar at the same time. It was in such a "weight/wait of time" that this book was conceived. In 1990, a month before my long awaited oral defense for my Ph.D. in psychology, I was diagnosed with a viral induced ventricular tachycardia. V. Tach., also called "sudden death syndrome," was the first step on my journey into the "weight of time."

The experience of knowing I had a life-threatening illness and the immediate necessity of discovering ways of living with this diagnosis forced me to find coping strategies required of anyone who would be a "wounded storyteller." Some of the coping strategies to which I attribute my healing were the following: excellent medical care, faithful and loving family and friends, psychological/emotional support, and spiritual support. Without all these systems, finding meaning in this trauma would have been impossible. In gratitude for my good fortune, I decided to use this information to assist others on a similar healing journey.

In 1994 a small group of dedicated professionals from different religious and cultural backgrounds came together by invitation once a month to pray, reflect, and develop a program to assist others dealing with life-threatening illness, loss, and death. Partners in Healing was born. Given the dramatic changes in the health care delivery system and its implications for shortened hospital stays, and given the rising numbers of frail elderly persons in our communities, it seemed that the time was right to develop a program to train and support volunteers. This would be done in collaboration with other health care providers, religious groups, educational facilities, and community organizations to help professionals and lay people explore the challenges of illness, aging, loss, and death by bringing spiritual, emotional, and psychological comfort to those in need as a way of participating in the healing process.

In 1995 and again 1996 meetings were held with religious and community leaders to present the content of the program and to ascertain if this approach met the needs of the people who were suffering. Religious and community leaders fully endorsed the Partners in Healing program. With their blessing, an eight-week program of training was offered in 1997 to members of the Universal Baptist Church in the Bedford Stuyvesant section of Brooklyn; the second pilot program was offered in 1998 at Saint Francis Xavier Church in Manhattan.

The pilot program was based on four support systems: spiritual, medical, psychological, and social. The topics covered in the eight-week training program for volunteers were the following: (1) Companions of hope, (2) Empathic listening, (3) Role of presence in the relationship, (4) The systemic implications of illness and loss, (5) Medical considerations, (6) Ethical concerns, (7) Spiritual care of the sick, and (8) Theology of hope.

This book reflects the importance of focusing on the care partner, the pastoral volunteer. Each chapter is written by a member of Partners in Healing. The authors bring their own creativity and passion to the topics as they explore the ministry of visiting the sick and the bereaved. The editors did not try to meld the individual "voices" into a seamless garment; thus, the reader will find a diversity of style, content, and spirituality expressed in the various chapters.

The book is divided into three parts. The first part deals with the meaning of illness. John R. Bickle endeavors to assist the patient and the volunteer find meaning in the experience of loss. Then Elizabeth M. Renyi speaks with the powerful voice of a patient and clarifies the role of spouse and family members in the healing process.

The second part of the book deals with specific issues that will be encountered by visitors. My three chapters on empathy and on presence stand alone and at the same time relate to the entire book; the spirit of presence and empathy as well as the importance of focusing on the role of the care partners is at the heart of all chapters. Two excellent hospital chaplains, Sarah L. Fogg and Curtis W. Hart, offer clarity of thinking and practical advice that is essential for volunteers who visit patients. Kathleen M. Duffy, a professional nurse as well as a lay parish minister, touches on the health issues that visitors must be aware of, and Jacqueline C. Perez, a physician, reflects on encounters that are healing for the patient's body and spirit.

The final section of the book deals with issues involved in setting up and sustaining visitation programs. Patricia Cusack, O.P., speaks of the recruitment and training of volunteers. Elizabeth A. Baker discusses the kind of support needed to sustain a volunteer group and the healing process that occurs in the group context. Michelle D. White brings the book to a close by explaining the practical applications and possible difficulties in creating a pastoral visitation program.

The path of a pastoral volunteer, a care partner, is one that demands courage and resilience. It is a journey of hope and, for the pastoral volunteer, it is an ongoing road to Emmaus. We can walk this path because we do not walk it alone. He goes before us. He walks with us.

PART I
The Meaning of Illness

The Spiritual Pain of Illness: Finding Meaning in Loss

John R. Bickle

> "I was ill and you comforted me."
> (Matthew 25:36)

Health care providers recently identified pain as the fifth vital sign. In addition to the four vital signs of temperature, blood pressure, heart rate, and respiration, patients are asked to identify their level of pain, and health care personnel are required to work to alleviate that pain. It is important to note that pain is not merely a physical phenomenon, but involves the whole person: body, mind, and spirit. Although the methods to alleviate physical and emotional pain have improved in recent years, few resources have been allocated to address the *spiritual* pain experienced by those who are ill. Chaplains, trained professional spiritual caregivers, are often absent or in short supply at many health care institutions. Few medical schools train physicians on methods or the value of spiritual assessment. Although many nursing schools instruct students on the importance of assessing and addressing the spiritual needs of patients (indeed, most research in this area has been conducted by nurses), reductions in nursing staffs and the shortened length of patient stays often prohibit nurses from doing a spiritual assessment. Even in those few institutions with adequate staffing of chaplains, because of the increasing financial pressure to shorten patient length of stays, the spiritual needs of patients remain largely ignored. Chaplains often do not even meet patients!

The burden of assessing and addressing the spiritual needs of the sick has increasingly fallen to overworked and understaffed parish clergy or to poorly trained and ill-equipped volunteers. The purpose of this chapter is *not* to transform a visitor into a trained professional chaplain, but to help increase the comfort level of the visitor when encountering those who are experiencing spiritual pain. Although we may not be professionally trained, we are all, to some extent, spiritual caregivers for each other. Self-knowledge, or discovering how we might respond to serious illness in our own lives, can help us become more actively present to those whom we encounter in our visits to the sick. As we learn what meanings *we* might ascribe to illness, we can become more attuned to the experiences of *others*. We can become fellow travelers with them, accompanying them on their journey.

Spirituality for our purposes is defined in the broadest possible context: the *meaning* given to persons, places, and events in our lives. What meanings do people give to the event of illness, injury, or disease? Because of a lack of personal experience with serious illness, visitors are often uncomfortable encountering those who are seriously ill. How would I react? How could I cope? What would this mean for me if I were stricken? All of these questions can surface when meeting those who are ill. How *do* people react to serious illness? How *do* people cope? The scriptures reveal to us a number of possible "meanings" ascribed to illness. Each one of these "meanings" can be framed as a function of *loss:* loss of independence or autonomy, loss of certainty, and loss of perception. Familiarizing ourselves with these reactions to illness as recounted in the scriptures can be helpful.

Illness as Punishment/Loss of Autonomy

"There is no health in my flesh because of your indignation"; "Noisome and festering are my sores because of my folly; . . . there is no health in my flesh" (Psalm 38:3, 6, 7); "But if you do not hearken to the voice of the Lord, . . . the Lord will bring a pestilence upon you, . . . will strike you with wasting and fever" (Deuteronomy 28:15, 21–22); "Because you have not followed the path of your father

... the Lord will strike you ... with a great plague; and you shall have severe pains from a disease in your bowels" (2 Chronicles 21:12, 14–15).

These are but a few of the numerous scriptural references to illness, disease, pestilence, plague, and even death that result directly from our failure to adhere to the commandments of the Lord. Simply put, this view maintains that if you observe the Lord's commands, you shall be rewarded with prosperity and good health; if you fail to heed the Lord's commands, you shall be punished with poverty and sickness, even death. In secular terms, we would describe this view as one that sees illness as "behaviorally induced," that is, as sickness that arises as a direct result of one's actions or failure to act. Such a person might be the smoker who is diagnosed with lung cancer, the obese person with blocked arteries who failed to restrict her diet, or the person who suffers from a sexually transmitted disease. It represents a mathematically concise world-view, an "if this, then that" approach. It is often expressed as "I deserved this."

Once, while making rounds as a chaplain, I met a patient named Bill who had been admitted to the hospital after testing positive for HIV and who was being treated for numerous opportunistic infections. Bill welcomed my visit as chaplain and explained to me that he had been raised in a fundamentalist tradition. "I guess it's true that we reap what we sow," he said. I listened as he detailed his theological beliefs, his claim that his illness was indeed a punishment from God, that he had failed to observe the Lord's commands regarding sexual activity outside of marriage. In return, God had delivered this curse upon him. There was no anger in this declamation; instead, there was almost a resigned acceptance that he had "gotten what he deserved." The fundamental meaning that Bill had given to his illness was that he was being justifiably punished for his offenses. He had lost his sense of independence or autonomy. The situation was beyond his control.

Illness as Mystery/Loss of Certainty

"Your hands have formed me and fashioned me; will you then turn and destroy me?" (Job 10:8); "My God, my God, why have you forsaken me, far from my prayer, from the words of my cry?" (Psalm 22:1); "Why, then, should you forget us, abandon us so long a time?" (Lamentations 5:20); "Yet when I looked for good, then evil came; when I expected light, then came darkness" (Job 30:26); "Then toward midafternoon Jesus cried out in a loud tone, *'Eli, Eli, lema sabachtani?'* that is, 'My God, my God, why have you forsaken me?'" (Matthew 27:46).

Perhaps the clearest expression of illness as mystery is contained in the Book of Job. A righteous man, Job is suddenly beset with multiple miseries. He loses his wealth, his family, and his health. Contrary to the popular expression, he is not patient but, rather, demands to know why all of this has befallen him. His well-intentioned friends insist he must have done something to deserve these afflictions, but Job repeatedly asserts that there can be no rational explanation for his sufferings. His experience can best be summed up in the expression: "Why is this happening to me?"

Mary had recently been admitted to the hospital, diagnosed with end-stage lung cancer. When I met her, she explained to me that she had always taken good care of herself. She never smoked, rarely drank, watched her diet, and exercised regularly. She observed that she had tried to be a good role model for her three grown children, and was proud that they had followed her example of healthy living. "When the doctor told me I had lung cancer, I was certain there must be a mistake," she said. "I couldn't believe it." Mary went to Mass regularly and revealed that she found herself repeating a one-word prayer, "Why?" "I just keep asking the same question, over and over: Why? Why is this happening to me? And I get no answers," she claimed. Like Job, Mary could find no reason for her suffering. Her illness was a mystery. She had lost her sense of certainty about the way the world "worked."

Illness as Ultimate Good/Loss of Perception

"As he walked along, [Jesus] saw a man who had been blind from birth. His disciples asked him, "Rabbi, was it his sin or that of his parents that caused him to be born blind?" "Neither," answered

Jesus: "It was no sin, either of this man or of his parents. Rather it was to let God's works show forth in him" (John 9:1–3); "Yet it was our infirmities that he bore, our sufferings that he endured, While we thought of him as stricken, as one smitten by God and afflicted. But he was pierced for our offenses, crushed for our sins, Upon him was the chastisement that makes us whole, by his stripes we were healed" (Isaiah 53:4–5); "I suffer as a criminal . . . I bear with all of this for the sake of those whom God has chosen" (2 Timothy 2:9–10); "I am content with weakness, with mistreatment, with distress, with persecutions and difficulties for the sake of Christ" (2 Corinthians 12:10); "Even now I find my joy in the suffering I endure for you. In my own flesh I fill up what is lacking in the sufferings of Christ for the sake of his body, the church" (Colossians 1:24).

The Judeo-Christian tradition maintains that any human suffering is objectively evil. Moreover, we are obliged to alleviate the sufferings of our fellow human beings whenever possible. But the scriptures reveal to us that human suffering can lead to a positive outcome. For Christians, the suffering, death, and resurrection of Jesus give profound new meaning to the experience of pain in our lives. There is a transforming power available to the believer, a power that is patterned after the salvific actions of Jesus himself. Pain and suffering remain evil, but the experience can be infused with the same meaning as the redemptive acts of Jesus: suffering and death lead to new life and hope. We are not speaking of some sadomasochistic desire to luxuriate in human misery. Rather, the suffering that all persons experience simply because of their humanity can become a source for good. It can be transfigured.

Within the first few weeks of my ministry as a hospital chaplain, I met Jim. Jim was being treated for a collapsed lung, secondary to HIV. This was his third hospitalization for the same ailment. Even though he had difficulty speaking, Jim wanted me to hear his story. Describing himself as "not very religious," Jim told me that he was in his late twenties, married, and had been diagnosed with AIDS a few months prior to our meeting. During high school, Jim had begun to experiment with drugs. Seeking ever greater highs, he soon became addicted to heroin. "I woke up one morning literally lying in the gutter," he remembered. "That day I called and asked my family for help. They got me into a treatment facility. It was like boot camp. We had to do things like clean the shower stalls with a toothbrush."

Six months later, Jim began his new life clean and sober. He got a good job where he met his future wife. "A few months after we got married, I got a cold that wouldn't go away," he said. "I finally went to my family doctor. He knew my drug history. I was shocked when he suggested I get tested for HIV. I hadn't used heroin for several years at that point. I got tested and, sure enough, the test came back positive." He paused for a moment. "I was devastated. The hardest part was telling my wife. I was sure she would want to leave me. She hadn't bargained for this," he mused.

Jim continued his story, recounting how his wife reminded him that she had married him for better or worse, in sickness and in health. "She's the breadwinner now," he said. "She's here every day after work and she brings me food from home." Tears came to his eyes. "I deserved this. I mean, I didn't know there was a risk for AIDS when I was sharing needles, but, hey, I knew it wasn't healthy. But my wife tested positive. She's not sick or anything, but, what did she ever do to deserve this?" he asked.

At this point, Jim echoed both Bill's and Mary's sentiments regarding his illness. He "deserved" this because of his acknowledged drug use, and at the same time he was asking "why" his wife had become infected. Illness was both "punishment" and "mystery." Jim's sense of self-control and his certitude about the way things should be had been challenged. But his story wasn't finished.

I continued to meet with Jim and his wife over the next several weeks. New to the area, I had become increasingly aware of the lack of community resources for persons with AIDS. The nearest support group was located more than fifty miles away. One evening Jim raised the subject. "I wonder if there are other people like me? You know, shocked by the news, trying to be a good husband, wondering what will happen. What treatments are available. Things like that."

I explained that I had investigated local resources and discovered that the nearest support group where persons with AIDS did in fact get together to share their experiences was in the northern part of the state. "Well, then, I guess I'll just have to start one here," he announced. "The worst part for me when I got the news was the feeling of being alone. I mean, my wife was there, for sure. But the two of us didn't know what to do, who to tell, who to call, where to go. I wouldn't want anyone else to feel like that."

Several weeks later, with the help of a social worker, Jim founded the first support group in the area for persons newly diagnosed with HIV. He continued to lead and participate in this group until his death two years later. The group continues to this day, having expanded its services to those with chronic illness, as well as providing support for caregivers. Jim was able to transform the objective evil of his illness into a source of good for others. He had lost his previously held belief that nothing good could possibly come from this. He found positive meaning in the experience of his illness, recognizing that the needs of others at the time of their diagnosis would be similar in nature to what his had been. By helping his neighbor, Jim let "God's work show forth in him."

What Visitors Can Do

As a part of their training, chaplains emphasize a growth in self-knowledge. They are asked to articulate a personal theology that includes the meaning of illness and human suffering. Who is the God to whom they pray? How have they dealt with illness in their own lives? What meanings did they ascribe to the experience? There is a twofold purpose here: (1) the ability to express one's own experience of illness can aid others in giving voice to their experience; and (2) by knowing our own experience, we can avoid projecting that experience onto others. We can "do good," and we can "do no harm."

As a visitor to those who are ill, you are not expected to have the same skill set as a professionally trained chaplain. However, all of us can benefit from the same self-reflection. As mentioned above, many people, including chaplains, are uncomfortable when first encountering those with serious, chronic, or life-threatening illnesses. This lack of comfort stems in part from a lack of personal experience with serious injury or disease. Despite this void, however, there are some ways to develop insight into how one might react to illness, how one might reasonably predict the meanings one might ascribe to the experience of sickness. As described above, those who are ill experience numerous losses: loss of independence, loss of certainty, loss of perception and self-identity, loss of functions, loss of employment, loss of housing, loss of some relationships, even the prospective loss of life itself. Although we may not have lived through a serious or chronic illness, all of us have certainly experienced loss: loss of a loved one, a relationship, a pet, a job, a precious object, etc. Examining how we reacted to these losses in our lives, the meanings we ascribed to the experiences, how we coped with losses, what "worked" for us, what did not "work," can help us begin to identify some of the processes a person who is sick may be going through. The following exercise may help.

On a sheet of paper draw a horizontal line. Starting from the left, write the number zero, then write the number five, and then, in increments of five, continue writing numbers up to your current age. Beginning at the left point of this horizontal line, draw a vertical line upward and, beginning at the bottom, write the numbers one to ten. It should look something like this:

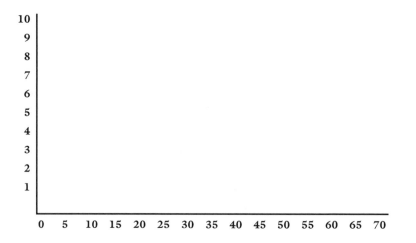

Take a few moments to reflect on your life experiences. What losses have you encountered? How old were you when they occurred? After you have identified several losses in your life, find the age at which they occurred and draw an "x" above the age to rate the level of pain (10 is equal to the most severe pain). Do this for each remembered occurrence.

Review each "x." Which meaning(s) did you attach to these loss experiences: 1—Punishment ("I deserved this"); 2—Mystery ("Why is this happening to me?"); or 3—Source of Ultimate Good ("Something good came from this experience")? Write the corresponding numbers near each "x." Remember that you may have found multiple meanings in one experience. Is there a pattern for the more painful losses? Have your perceptions changed over time? Did you respond to similar events differently? How did these events change your relationships? Was your prayer life altered? Answering these questions has predictive value. It can give you greater insight into how you may respond to serious illness in your own life. It can also give you insight into the experience of those you are visiting.

The final part of the exercise is an analysis of our coping skills. We obviously survived these losses in our lives. What got us through them? People respond differently and uniquely to the same stimuli. Some seek out others when they are in pain, finding comfort in sharing the experience with those willing and able to listen. Others find solace in isolation, retreating to their "hermitage." Many turn to quiet, prayerful reflection, using the "down time" of illness or loss to reconnect with their God. Others may engage in "scream therapy," that is, cursing the darkness of illness and loss, loudly lamenting the experience. Some people try to deaden their pain by turning to anesthetics: prescription pain medication, alcohol, street drugs, sex. Others find the experience of pain a positive sign of their continued existence: if I feel pain, I know I'm alive. To illustrate some of these coping styles, let's return to the stories of Bill and Mary.

Bill—the "I deserved this" fundamentalist—continued to welcome my visits. I noted that as his hospitalization lengthened, he had fewer visitors. His family flew in once from the Midwest and stayed for a long weekend, but his friends seemed to come to the hospital less frequently and stay for shorter times. I asked him how he felt about this and he replied with a one-word answer: "Lonely." Bill had told me earlier of a positive experience he had had with a church community in the area. I asked him if he wanted me to contact the minister, and he said yes. He was somewhat hesitant, because he had never acknowledged his illness or his sexuality to the pastor, but now he felt that it was the right time. When I called the church, the pastor was surprised to learn that Bill was a patient, and that he had been hospitalized for several weeks. He agreed to come. After the minister's visit, I asked Bill how it had gone. "He was wonderful," Bill said. "I told him everything, and he just hugged me." The pastor connected Bill with the church's prayer line and asked if he would like visitors from the community's pastoral visitors group. Bill said he would, and every day for the rest of his hospitalization Bill was visited by members of his faith community. They shared the scriptures, prayed together, and sang familiar hymns. Bill's mood improved. He no longer spoke of deserving his illness, but repeatedly asserted how God's love was reflected in these visitors. "When they hug me at the beginning and end of their visits, I feel as if God has hugged me," he remarked. He observed that, although he wished he hadn't become ill, he was thankful for the gift of time his illness had brought him: time to reflect on his life, his relationships, and his God.

Mary, the "Why is this happening to me?" patient, asked to be left alone. "We had a dog once who was hit by a car. She was seriously hurt, and it took a long time for her to recover. When she came home from the vet's, she would often go into a room by herself. I'd discover her literally licking her wounds," she observed. "I need time to do just that." Respecting Mary's wishes, I would only occasionally pop in just to say hello and ask how she was doing. One day, in answer to my question, she replied, "I think it's time for me to leave my cave." She explained that her favorite saint, Francis of Assisi, had often retreated to caves to pray and reflect on his life and the mystery of God. Refreshed and renewed, he would then return to his active ministry of preaching and proclaiming the Good News. "I'm ready to face the world now," she stated simply. "I needed this time for myself. I'm glad I had the chance to think about things, how I want to deal with all this. I used to think, 'Why me, Lord?' Now I think, 'Why not me?'"

Bill, Mary, and Jim all faced serious illness. Each ascribed different meanings to the experience. Each experienced loss of one kind or another. Each coped in unique ways. If you are seriously considering volunteering to visit those who are sick, it is essential that you maintain a stance of openness toward those you visit. It is equally essential that you develop the facility to articulate your own experience of loss and your coping ability. Professional spiritual caregivers engage in a practice called "peer-review," seeking out others in their profession to assist them in identifying personal issues that may have an impact on the care they deliver. This is a good practice for volunteers as well. Share your stories of loss with other visitors. Listen to their stories. What do you have in common with others? What differences do you find? Perhaps most important, acknowledge what it is like to know that you have been heard. Allowing people to tell their stories, refraining from interrupting, stopping oneself before giving advice are all essential in creating an environment where healing can begin.

Again, you are not expected to become a chaplain. When you find yourself in a situation where you do not know how to proceed, be sure that you know where to turn: to your pastor, your group facilitator, or a chaplain. Never hesitate to ask for assistance. When others share with us their intimate concerns, their fears and hopes, their dreams and nightmares, we have come upon "holy ground." We honor this sacred space when we acknowledge our limitations. We become more actively present to those we visit when we gently refer them to persons more qualified to assist them.

As a visitor to those who are ill, you will undoubtedly encounter people in spiritual pain. Being open to the possible "spiritual reactions" to illness, the unique ways people cope with loss in their lives, is essential in this ministry. Develop active listening skills. As you become increasingly aware of your own spiritual journey, as you improve your facility to articulate a spirituality uniquely your own, you can be better equipped to assist others on their way. You will be a fellow traveler, one who indeed knows the meaning of Jesus' words: "I was ill and you comforted me."

For Further Reading

Ahronheim, J., & Weber, D. (1992). *Final Passages: Positive Choices for the Dying and Their Loved Ones.* New York: Simon & Schuster.

Dossey, L. (1996). *Prayer Is Good Medicine: How to Reap the Healing Benefits of Prayer.* New York: HarperCollins.

Holst, L. (1985). *Hospital Ministry: The Role of the Chaplain Today.* New York: Crossroad.

Koenig, H. (1999). *The Healing Power of Faith: Science Explores Medicine's Last Great Frontier.* New York: Simon & Schuster.

Matthews, D. (1998). *The Faith Factor: Proof of the Healing Power of Prayer.* New York: Viking.

New American Bible: Saint Joseph Edition (1970). American Bible Pub. Co.

Sulmasy, Daniel (1997). *The Healer's Calling: A Spirituality for Physicians and Other Health Care Professionals.* Mahwah, N.J.: Paulist Press.

The Spiritual Challenge of Illness: Hope

Elizabeth M. Renyi

Introduction

This chapter will look at the relational and faith dynamics of illness. Personal experiences and theological reflection will be used to show how societal and faith support systems can lead us to feel a healing sense of hope. Hope happens when one comes to accept illness and to feel peace with this acceptance. Then one is able to integrate illness into one's sense of self and accept the illness as part of one's being. The spiritual challenge of illness is to be able to continue to grow and to be healed. We can heal only in and with the presence of the other. We can heal only when we are in relationship.

Whether one is a caregiver, a friend, a casual visitor, or a member of the health care field, one can learn how easy it is to partner another in healing. Our supportive systems lead us on a faith journey involving an acceptance of illness. In a culture that often lacks close family ties, a sense of community, and where health care systems are generally non-supportive, we need to understand how important it is to be present and help partner others in their journey.

Faith Reflection

Our Christian faith calls us to be "in relationship"—with ourselves, with others, and with God. Christian spirituality implies these relationships; it encompasses all of our being. Our spirituality is a personal response that is continually being influenced by our culture.

It will change and grow in the context of our changing lives and relationships. In turn, these same relationships, or the lack of them, will directly influence our capacity and ability to heal. Illness directly affects our spirituality and the ability to heal, because it challenges and affects these relationships. All these relationships are necessary to develop a sense of hope.

Hope is essential to our human condition; it is an outlook and attitude that shapes all of our experience. It enables us to envision new possibilities, being driven by our will but conceived out of our actions. According to Irish theologian Dermot Lane, "Hope takes 'energy' to act...Hope arises from within the person—but only as an encounter with the exterior world of human beings...for the human to exist always means to co-exist and that to be is always to be in relationship." This sense of hope arises from all the relationships within our support systems. It comes from our sense of empowerment/control and from the coping skills that we ourselves and those supporting us have. Most important, hope arises from our ability to interact and maintain relationships even while dealing with illness.

Illness threatens our sense of self. It directly challenges our self-image and threatens to strip away our personality, "our self." It strikes deeply to our core and strips away all the "fluff" in our lives. My own experience of illness struck me to my core, threatening my very being as I knew it. As I proceeded through my own journey of illness and grew deeper in my faith, two theologians spoke to me and offered meaning that energized me from within. The writings of Protestant theologian Paul Tillich touched my personal faith. In his book, *The Courage to Be,* he states that only through crises can our faith mature. Our doubt will affect our old relationship with God, but only so that a new relationship may develop. Says Tillich, "The courage to be is rooted in the God who appears when God has disappeared in the anxiety of doubt." During a crisis of illness, we search for meaning in our lives; we search for our "anchor places." Tillich's theology spoke to me only toward the end of my illness, when I had the time to pause and reflect back on the faith journey I had been led through.

The second theologian whose works spoke to me is Karl Rahner. His works express the communal nature of the experience of the

Spirit of God. It was the recognition of this communal nature that opened many graced moments to me and helped me move to a deeper faith. Rahner's writings speak especially to those who are ill and those who are partners in their healing. There are several points that are relevant to our relationships during illness. First, Rahner says, God offers himself to each person and is present in our very conscious experiences. If the effects of grace are real, then they can be felt within all our everyday activities of life, in the midst of our concrete world. "Our humanity exists in this world, thus God's grace must affect us in our everyday encounters," according to Rahner scholar Roger Haight. This everyday communication of God exists in our world; grace is a personal union with God acting in the present moment. Thus, the graced moments of life, the making of God's presence visible, are found only in our relationships. In illness, when we are stripped to our core, we can become receptive to so many moments of grace. It is an opportunity in which God's presence can be revealed to us.

There was a moment in the very beginning of my illness that will remain with me forever. If God was ever in my life, it was at this instant, and, luckily, I recognized it. I had been told twenty-four hours earlier that I would be paralyzed from the C-5 vertebra down, due to arthritis (anklylosing spondylitis), and that it was not likely that anything could be done about it. I was to see a neurosurgeon the next day. During the twenty-four hours of waiting, I was terror-stricken. I knew all too well what might lie ahead. I had grown up in a family where my mother was confined to a wheelchair, incapaci-tated with rheumatoid arthritis. I could only envision worse for myself—with no feeling, no movement, and no control. As I was about to go in for my first appointment with the neurosurgeon, my husband looked at me and said, "Just remember, no matter what the doctor tells us, we will still have fun." To me, that meant more than love; it meant a life. I felt instantly that it was a graced moment. It struck me deeply, right to my core, which had been laid bare by the threat to my being. A simple comment, "we will still have fun," reaffirmed my being and started me on a journey with hope.

Systemic Reflection: Partnered Relationships

There are many and varied relationships in which a person becomes involved. When we refer to these relationships or "systems," we must begin with ourselves and look outward to all the other relational interactions that might influence us, such as family/caregivers, friends/community, health care network, medical facilities, social class, and culture. Our faith and beliefs also constitute an important system. These systems, in which we belong and with which we interact, directly influence how we cope with illness. Since they also directly influence and shape our attitude toward illness, we need to understand them. When there is illness, our relational systems must adjust and adapt in order to become supportive. Illness is not "business as usual." One's coping skills need to adjust to the new stress of illness. Our systems are empowering and supportive when they are able to adapt and be flexible, to offer options and choices. When they do, they make the difference between hope and hopelessness.

One can be an agent of hope simply by one's actions, concerns, and efforts. People who experience illness are initially afraid of not having support from their relational systems. It is only later that they express a fear of not getting support from their belief systems. As a partner in healing, one needs to understand the unique feelings of the individual who is experiencing illness and discern the role—whether supportive or non-supportive—that each of the individual's systems is playing. It takes very little to be supportive: perhaps just a simple word, a simple action, or a minute of listening.

The systems we belong to are the network of all of our relationships, from the intimate to the most distant or occasional interaction. Each of our social bonds has the potential to aid in our healing, because in all of them we find the source of our self-affirmation. Our relationships give us a sense of empowerment, a sense of security and control, and a sense of being connected to a larger social network. To partner another person in illness requires a sense of presence and awareness to the other in relationship. As a partner or visitor, one needs to be aware that very often one will be present with another at some of the most despairing moments of his or her life. Arthur

Frank, in his book *Wounded Storyteller,* explains that ill people need to tell their stories of illness in order to reconstruct their disrupted relationships. When people tell their stories, as the illness evolves, they begin to make the illness a part of their lives. The families, visitors, and those closest to the ill person are in the unique position of allowing these stories to be told.

Societal Influences

As a partner or a visitor, you need to understand the influence that society and culture have on the person experiencing illness. You must be aware that you may harbor your own cultural feelings toward the ill. We live in a culture that places great emphasis on beauty and self-sufficiency. In today's society, success is defined in ways that glorify autonomy, independence, and self-sufficiency. Our culture values beauty and youth, all the while viewing the physical body as a potent symbol of selfhood. Cultural expectations have to do with our control of our lives and with individual achievements. These expectations are very disturbing for a person who experiences illness. When one becomes "sick," social expectations change. The sick person is isolated and often socially marginalized. When we label someone as sick, we have the power to discredit him or her, for illness often carries negative connotations that are far worse than the condition itself. Often, depending on the gender or class of the person, the same sickness may have different connotations: think of AIDS, tuberculosis, leprosy, or sexually transmitted diseases. The social stigma of illness not only touches one's family and close friends but also affects all the relationships the ill person has.

Financial status is another factor that can influence the development of a sense of hope. Individuals and families with economic problems have limited access to supportive relationships within society. Such people may already have been socially isolated prior to the onset of illness. Reflect on the advantages that financial resources afford us in times of illness, for instance the access to and the choice of doctors and medical facilities. Most of the population does not have this freedom of choice.

There's another silent cultural factor inherent within our medical system that impedes a sense of hope. The ill person seeking medical help is in an intrinsically inferior position because of the social distance built into the "expert-to-layperson" relationship. This is apparent in the doctor-patient relationship and in managed care systems. It often results in poor communication and a lack of empathy toward the person experiencing illness. The greater the social distance, the less sensitivity each side will feel for the other's circumstances. Medical personnel can cause unnecessary suffering when they fail to give clear and adequate information. Distress can easily be felt in trying to deal with the bureaucratic maze of one's managed care plans, especially when it's laid on top of the illness itself.

The Evolution of Hope

The evolution of a feeling of hope greatly depends upon receiving adequate information, along with the control it offers. Relationships that inhibit faith development and inhibit the feeling of hope are those that offer no voice, no medical opportunities, and no feeling of empowerment. When we believe our illness is personal, permanent, and pervasive, we feel totally hopeless. The very first news of my illness came through a phone call from the doctor who had ordered my MRI. The results were totally unexpected, and he relayed the following message to me: Don't move, don't do this or that . . . "because we are talking about paralysis from the neck down. It's probably due to your arthritis and can't be fixed. We need to get you to a neurosurgeon as soon as possible." His news was personal, permanent, and pervasive. He made it sound like I had few options and little control. It gave me the feeling that my situation was hopeless—and this came from a doctor who is normally one of the most supportive, sensitive, and compassionate people I know. At that instant the news appeared so dire to him that he merely passed along the words of the radiologist. This shows how easily a sense of hopelessness can be conveyed. On the other hand, the very first words I received from the neurosurgeon were simply: "We can fix this, but first more tests are needed."

To feel a sense of hope, we need to be able to approach an illness as a situation that offers options—whether it involves a choice of treatment or the kind of supportive care we'll be getting. To feel hope, we need to know that we have options and a voice in deciding how to deal with our illness.

Dynamics and Feelings of Illness

As we reflect on relationships and systems, we need to start with the person who is sick. Illness can be either acute or chronic. Acute illness is contained, runs its course, and is short-lived. With a chronic illness, one is threatened with steady deterioration, and medical treatment is centered on managing and controlling the deterioration over a long period of time. In chronic illness, there is a need for constant reevaluation. Chronic illness forces ill people to continually reassess and re-work the meanings of their altered lives. There is a constant sense of loss, an ongoing emotional readjustment. Chronic pain is a physical reminder that things are not right and may never be right again.

To appreciate and help the other in such a situation, the caregiver or visitor needs to understand the feelings and dynamics that result from experiencing illness. Because illness totally disrupts all of our relationships, our social norms and expectations, it imposes a temporary escape from normal role requirements. Imagine a wage earner or mother who becomes ill and can't function in the usual manner. The change in role can be devastating to that person's sense of self. It invariably puts stress on the entire family. It turns everyday existence into chaos. Normal family routine is changed as all the attention and energy becomes focused on the ill person. There is a loss of connectedness with family members, within social groups, and with our social role. The importance of having a partner in healing—whether a family member, a medical professional, or a pastoral visitor—is that such a partner can help to re-establish the vital sense of being connected. Families need to realize that they can help to maintain this sense of relation and help to give meaning to an individual's experience of illness.

Illness is a form of stress that begins with the person experiencing illness. It takes energy to be sick. Illness demands a change within the sick person and in all his or her relationships. When trying to cope with illness, the family system needs to be flexible and adjust to different family role responsibilities. Because my mother was incapacitated by arthritis, my father had to hold a full-time job and then come home at night to do most of the things a mother would do—shop for food, run errands, clean the house. Since there were no financial resources for outside help, we simply had to adapt and adjust. We learned very quickly that things got done only if we all pitched in to help.

People who are ill experience many different feelings. They don't come all at once but surface at different stages during the progression of the illness. But all the feelings must be experienced if the ill person is going to come to a state of acceptance and peace. Let me share a few of the feelings I experienced during my journey. Initially, there was the trauma of illness. One minute I was fine, and in the next minute, my life, as I knew it, was threatened. The question immediately arose: "What am I going to do?" Everything follows from this question. The trauma of illness lays the self bare; it strikes us to the core, peeling away our defenses. I felt naked and vulnerable. I focused on that which Tillich refers to as one's "ultimate concern." Immediately I began to wonder: What life would I have totally paralyzed? Would it really be a life? Who was I going to be when I had no feeling or movement in my body? What self-image would I have if I lost control of my bodily functions and became totally dependent on others? Part of my life's dream was to experience life actively in a family setting. Suddenly this dream was threatened. I became totally absorbed with the impact this would have on me and on my family. From my childhood experience, I knew firsthand how a family needed to adjust and what daily sacrifices it took to raise a family in such circumstances. I was acutely aware of the changes that would be necessary and the stresses that would develop as a result. I could imagine the feelings of isolation that illness would bring. I remembered my mom's struggle to stay connected to her outside world, to maintain outside relationships that provide the connectedness she needed. My mother would constantly reach out to stay connected. Whatever she could do from home, such as telephoning, she volunteered to do. A eucharistic minister from her church not only kept her connected to her faith but would stay for coffee afterward and chat about happenings in the parish. So simple but yet so meaningful!

I certainly experienced anger and denial. I had already accepted, integrated, and was living with my chronic illness—the ankylosing spondylitis. However, I hadn't bargained for this added development. I had never been told it was a possibility. I just couldn't believe that something like what had happened to my mother was happening to me. I was especially angry because I had a young family; my husband's career was taking off, with attendant opportunities for all of us. It wasn't fair—I had so much to do! My initial faith reaction was the typical: How could this be? What God would do this to me? I always thought I had faith: after all, I regularly attended Mass, taught religion class, and both my husband and I were eucharistic ministers. Suddenly I experienced Doubt with a capital D. Only later, reflecting on my journey, did I understand Tillich's reference to the role of crises in one's faith development.

Illness produces a feeling of isolation—both emotionally and physically. There is an immediate loss of connectedness with those around you. I could no longer relate to others in the usual ways. I went through the daily routine thinking, "Oh, how I wish it were last week, going to those soccer games. I'll never complain again! Just get me back to my normal life!" In situations such as this, when attention is focused on the ill person, he or she begins to feel separate from the daily activities going on all around. It takes time to realize that illness has become part of your life, and it takes more time to adjust to that fact. One vivid memory remains with me during this initial period of my illness. While I was grappling with what my life might end up being, the rest of the world continued as if nothing had happened. How dare it! Two days before my first scheduled spinal surgery, I attended a fifth grade Parents' Back to School Night for my daughter. I could barely contain myself when seemingly the most important issue was to decide who was to bake the cupcakes for the various class celebrations during the year. I had all I could do not to stand up to shout "Are you serious?" It was more than I could stand.

During my illness, certain actions and words of friends and visitors offered me comfort, hope, and acknowledgment of what I was experiencing. The first was when my husband said that, no matter what, we would still have fun. Fun was an action word that held hope for me. My husband had no idea of what he was saying; it just came from his heart and proved to be a life-affirming comment. If God was in my life, I felt it immediately. Another comment was expressed a few minutes later by my neurosurgeon. While my problem was complicated and uncommon, he did reassuringly state that it could be fixed—he just had to figure out how! But the phrase "it can be fixed" naturally sent me on a high. All the fears and hopeless feelings of the previous twenty-four hours were lifted. Those words motivated me and kept me going for what turned out to be another three years. His words gave me a sense of empowerment and control.

On the other hand, some other comments were of no help at all, but left me feeling hollow or angry. Among these were statements that God would take care, or that God only gives you as much as you can handle. My response (silent of course) was to say: "What God? Right now I doubt God. Besides, God won't take care. I'm the one who has to deal with this." If the person had offered to pray that I would have strength to cope, I would have understood. Another comment I heard was: "It'll be all right." That's easy for another person to say, but it's *my* future that's at stake. Sorry, but I hadn't reached the point where I could feel that it would be all right. Another comment that never seemed to have meaning for me was to be told that I looked so good! I might have looked good, but I felt absolutely horrible, to say the least. I would be in pain and could hardly function and I would be told that I looked great! It would have been better to have simply acknowledged that I was in pain. It's always better to acknowledge that something is not right, because that's the truth! It's better to hear the worries, fears, and feelings related to that first question: "What am I going to do?" Remember, we all need to tell our stories, to be listened to and to be affirmed in what we are experiencing. I myself fell into saying very quickly to a friend just home from having a mastectomy that she looked so good. Well, she did—she was showered, dressed and about. But I caught myself as I was saying the words. I hugged her and said I truly did understand that she was feeling rotten and scared.

The Agent of Hope: The Caregiver

In the world of illness, one's caregiver is the primary partner for healing. He or she is an ill person's foremost support system. However, in the real world we know many ailing people are dealing with illness alone, without support. Friends and visitors should be aware of this fact. The quality of any care-giving relationship is of utmost importance. As with all of one's systems, care giving can be either supportive or non-supportive. It is not surprising to find that spouses or close family members have difficulty dealing with illness. They are not always so attentive or willing to share the feelings and emotions that illness calls forth. Two friends of mine who were struggling with the news of a cancer diagnosis had spouses that couldn't deal with the fact. One immersed himself in his work and told his wife that she should do what she had to alone. I sat with her the morning that she was trying to make a connection with a surgeon while her husband went off to work (as usual) so he wouldn't have to deal with it. The other spouse was very supportive, in his own way. He bought my friend a new car, but he couldn't share her worst fears or hold her at midnight when she most needed it. Nor would he take her to her chemotherapy. We all took turns sitting with her through her sessions. When situations such as these appear, it is especially important that a close friend or member of one's faith community provide care giving.

First and foremost, the ill person should receive affirmation from the care-giving partner. The caregiver should be able to acknowledge the presence of illness and the problems it brings. The ill person's feelings need to be acknowledged. A caregiver must hear and understand the feelings, fears, and concerns that stem from that question, "What am I going to do?" True care giving allows the ailing person to verbalize negative thoughts, and affirm that his or her fears are real. Care giving involves offering a sense of control, support, and companionship. A caregiver should be able to interface with other "systems" in the ill person's life, especially those in the medical area. By doing this, the caregiver provides a feeling of empowerment for the one coping with the illness. A caregiver should provide connections with the outside world; the partner can be the difference between a sense of being isolated and a sense of connectedness. A caregiver should be able to realize that new coping skills are needed—that the ill person will have to adapt and change in order to deal with the new stresses that have appeared.

I entered into my time of illness with strong coping skills acquired from my family of origin. My husband, my caregiver who set upon the journey with me, also had a great ability to change and cope. His coping skills had been fine-tuned from spending a year of Army service in Vietnam. Although I was not conscious at the time that we both had these skills, upon reflection I am able to see that they were there and how they evolved and supported our family and me.

My husband's comments and actions sustained in me a feeling of hope. From the very beginning, he said we would do it together, and, true to his word, we did it together. I was not lonely on this journey. My husband attended every doctor's appointment, every MRI session, every test, and every second opinion right through my last follow-up appointment. He sought out second opinions and set up appointments to learn more about my condition. He kept saying, "We'll do more" until we had an answer. At times when I was ready to give up in despair, his actions and support were very empowering. His care giving enabled me to feel that I had options, that I was not going to dead end in despair.

As a caregiver, my husband was always there to hear and understand my anger. He was there to hold me when I cried. He heard when I couldn't hear and he spoke when I couldn't speak. What he did, especially early on, was adapt, cope, and deal with all our "other systems." He interfaced with our family, friends, and the doctors. When I couldn't face talking about the ramifications of my spinal problems, he spoke to our three children. He kept our family on a path of normalcy. He didn't become burdened and overwhelmed; he adapted and coped. His Vietnam experience had taught him how to trust and endure. Now he was showing me.

Friends too added to that very vital sense of connectedness and affirmation. My usual responsibilities of shopping, errands, and car pooling the children were taken care of. The actions that had special meaning were those of friends who drove me to my graduate school classes, the friend who typed my papers because I was in too much pain to manage doing it myself, and the friend who came every afternoon to share coffee and the day. These seemingly simple gestures affirmed me and kept me connected. My ties were not broken.

In addition to my husband, the caregiver, my neurosurgeon also became an agent of hope for me. It was not only because of his initial comment, but because he was willing to be questioned by us, and he understood our need to obtain a second opinion. He referred us to other medical facilities, all the while sharing and offering all my medical records. Our economic situation enabled me to have choices, to keep searching for the right answer to address my problem. I was lucky to be able to have the top neurosurgeon at a world-renowned medical facility and to be given my choice of physicians. I did not have to cope with dealing with the bureaucracy of HMO's, worrying about financial resources or the coverage provided by health insurance. By citing my positive experience, I hope one can visualize what another might experience when there is no say or no choice, resulting in feelings of hopelessness. As partners in healing, we need to become aware of the supportive versus the non-supportive aspects of the other's life. I have highlighted, from personal reflection, hope-filled instances from my own experience. However, we need to be aware of the many people who are trying to deal with illness alone and without strong support systems. We can still partner them along in their journey through illness.

Conclusion

The integration or acceptance of illness involves recognizing the "aloneness of an illness" as opposed to feelings of "loneliness." While one does not need to be lonely on this journey, one must recognize that the illness is his or her own. Illness is a fact of one's life, not separate from it. It takes time to integrate illness into one's life. One needs to go through the darkness, through all the feelings and emotions that are experienced in illness. The ultimate question for the ill person is how to respond to new circumstances. This is a choice that everyone has. One needs to embrace illness, to accept it and to derive personal meaning from it. In order to come to a feeling of hope and healing, the individual must acknowledge that he or she alone must live with and accept the illness. In doing this, though, one must be helped along by partnered relationships.

Illness is both a spiritual challenge and a spiritual journey. It is a challenge to grow, to change, and be healed through acceptance of one's illness. Acceptance involves evolution, a journey of developing a new sense of self. It is the ability to "let go" of the old self in order to acknowledge a new one. It is the ability to surrender and trust, leading one to a Christian sense of resurrection. It is sensing the old self dying and coming to know a new sense of self. It is a feeling that "I can do this," and whatever happens all will be well. It is a journey of faith in which one realizes that all will be well with altered and new relationships. When these belief systems are felt, one can achieve a feeling of acceptance and peace.

We must discover our sources for supporting a sense of hopefulness —sources that are only found within all of our many and varied relationships. The ultimate challenge of illness is the self-affirmation derived through relationships—to oneself, to others, and to God.

For Further Reading

Frank, Arthur (1995). *Wounded Storyteller*. Chicago: University Press.

Freund, Peter E. S., & McGuire, Meredith, B. (1991). *Health, Illness and the Social Body*. Englewood Cliffs, N.J.: Prentice Hall.

Haight, Roger, S.J. (1979). *The Experience and Language of Grace*. New York: Paulist Press.

Lane, Dermot A. (1996). *Keeping Hope Alive: Stirrings in Christian Theology*. Mahwah, N.J.: Paulist Press.

Miller, William F., ed. (1999). *Integrating Spirituality into Treatment*. Washington, D.C.: American Psychological Association.

Rahner, Karl (1984). *The Practice of Faith*. New York: Crossroad.

Tillich, Paul (1952). *The Courage to Be*. New Haven: Yale University Press.

PART II
Issues for Visitors

Empathy: The Caregiver Looks Both Ways

Beverly Anne Musgrave

Introduction

If we believe that truly listening to another person is gift, gift for the receiver and gift for the giver, and if we believe in the mystery of the Incarnation and in what it bestows on human nature, then we have come close to believing in the mysterious movement which is at the heart of empathy. Moreover, in such belief, we can accept that the very "listening" itself is a way of seeing the face of Christ in another and listening to God in every genuine human encounter. The ability to truly listen to another human being and be present to that person—to be a self-in-relation—is the core experience of empathy.

Empathy is also an expression of "gracefulness" in the healing power of attentive presence, a "gracefulness" which in Christian understanding derives from the reality of incarnational blessing. It is an expression of grace, which is the divine presence in an act of true charity and genuine caring. This profound theological truth is beautifully and devoutly stated in the familiar hymn, *Ubi caritas et amor, Deus ibi est* ("Where charity and love prevail, God is ever there") which is surely a good description of what the pastoral visitation ought to be.

This chapter will expand on the definition of empathy and look at the complicated process of being empathic and using empathy skills so that they can facilitate the ministry of the visitor, which is essentially a ministry of presence, of active listening and attending to the sick and to the bereaved. It is my purpose to show that empathy skills facilitate ministerial presence and contribute to the experience of genuine human encounter. In a spiritual context, it is a means of grace or healing. And what takes place through the ministry of visiting is nothing less than bringing into human relationship the incarnational dimension of salvation, the "wholiness" or sacredness of the divine presence in Christian love.

The Art of Empathy

A celebrated Canadian photographer, Freeman Patterson, once said "the camera looks both ways." This was an insight into human nature that he most certainly learned from years of experience at his craft. His comment expresses his belief that there is a clear artistic connection between what takes place before the camera and what takes place behind it. The art of the photograph owes as much to one as to the other. Images photographed are as much a statement about the photographer as they are of the subject. Patterson believes the pictures we take are a documentation of our own personal history at the time the picture was taken. Through the camera, we see only what "the eye" records at that particular moment. The photograph reflects our ability to be present to a particular scene, person, or thing and our personal emotional response to it.

The wisdom of "the camera looks both ways" applies as well to the art of empathy. With Patterson, I believe that we cannot see anything until we are ready to see it, and I add that we cannot engage in empathic listening and genuine encounter until we are ready for it. The unique state of our unconscious life, the impact of our family of origin, the features of our cultural background, the conditions of our emotional and spiritual health all have a specific role to play in determining how we see and, I believe, in determining how we empathize.

Just as the camera looks both ways, so our ability to listen and empathize looks both ways. What we choose to hear, how we listen, and with whom we "empathize" are all statements about us. These statements shape our unique interior camera and give us a perspective, a lens through which we view others, and from that perspective we shape the response we choose to make.

Have you ever had the experience of listening to someone, a speaker, a politician, or a friend, and immediately feeling distress in your body? Or have you ever become aware that your cognitive perspectives—your ideas and values—were in strong disagreement with those of the speaker? How do you deal with such situations? As the person speaking to you expresses a contradictory belief system or an opposing attitude, your interior camera records a version modified by your own perspective and your internal emotion rejects an empathic response. If the speaker is someone who has no importance to you, you will block out the message and may not bother to listen. Then, of course, you will no longer be "bothered" by listening or by the speaker either.

If, on the other hand, the speaker is your spouse, your child, your colleague, or some other person who is important in your life, you'll feel the need to listen, to take that different point of view into consideration and to respond differently. To respond in an appropriate manner is not an easy thing to do. It is a great challenge. In the ministry of visiting, succeeding or failing to meet that challenge depends largely on the quality of listening and empathy skills the minister carries into the encounter.

People have great difficulty understanding different points of view and sometimes find it impossible to accept them. When the challenge for appropriate response is not met or is perceived to have failed, there is no genuine human encounter. The difficulty we have in understanding and accepting a different point of view or belief system is reflected in society at large. The news media—newspapers, magazines, television—provide daily accounts of the destructive consequences that follow the "disconnect" between human beings: various kinds of violence, structures of racial, sexual, and economic injustice, family disruptions from physical and psychological abuse.

Of particular concern for the ministry of healing and the ministry of the visitor are family relationships in which empathic listening and genuine human encounter are not always present. When some members of the family simply cannot understand or accept a different point of view or attitude, their typical response is to disconnect by refusing to speak to one another or to truly listen. There is no communication, no empathic presence. Family relationships become dysfunctional or lost altogether.

This same destructive process can occur in a close and intimate relationship of friendship. When a break in communication happens, one or the other friend may respond by leaving the relationship or by "cutting the other off." Most of us have known the stress and the pain of a broken relationship, of disaffection, of having trusted someone in friendship only to experience that trust not honored. However, by learning to be empathic, by taking the point of view of another and being present to that person in empathic response, we can hopefully stay in difficult relationships and heal them so that both parties value the differences that make them unique.

In her chapter "The Spiritual Challenge of Illness: Hope," Elizabeth Renyi discusses the systemic nature of illness and shows how the total family is affected. The systemic nature of the illness means that effects of the illness ripple into the lives of others. This often creates stress-filled moments for the family. In addition, relationships of the past are often brought into the present at a time of illness. This can be a matter of great importance for the patient and for the visitor as well.

Having relationships, past or present, in the family that are supportive and healing is wonderful for the person who is ill and for the other members as well. Sometimes, however, a visitor is asked to be attentive to the pain, loss, and hurt that need healing in a particular relationship or perhaps in several relationships. Realistically, the broken heart and the need for healing might belong not to the ill person but to another family member. Still, as partners in healing we are called to bring healing wherever it is needed. We are called to be attentive and to listen to people who may have very different perspectives from ours. This requires us to be aware of our own inner dynamics and to remember that we are seeing through one perspective the interior camera, so to speak, of our own belief system.

The best-selling book *Tuesdays with Morrie*, by Mitch Albom, is a wonderful and inspiring story and an example taken from life experience that demonstrates that the ministry of visiting is, to put it simply, a work of listening and empathic presence. Tuesdays were the one day each week the author dedicated to visit a man very close to death, his dear friend and professor, Morrie. In Mitch's later recollections of those visits, he came to understand in his own way that, during that time, the "camera looked both ways" and that he received as much from Morrie as he gave of himself. It was Morrie who was preparing himself to die, but during the days they spent together Mitch engaged in an ongoing struggle not only to listen to the words of a dying man but also to learn to walk the sacred journey toward death himself. I believe his determination to "walk this walk" was due in large part to his realization that "the camera looks both ways" and to his willingness to allow it to happen.

The Meaning of Empathy

For the purposes of this chapter, I will use this working definition of empathy: *Empathy is the ability to tolerate the tension of being truly open to the experience of another, the ability to attempt actively to understand the subjective world of the other and at the same time to remain a differentiated person.* To be empathic, one must be an active participant in a relationship, truly listening to and genuinely responding to another. When we are open to another person, a genuine dialogue can occur, a dialogue between the uniqueness of oneself and the uniqueness of the other. This dialogue is called being a self-in-relation. To be respectfully open to another involves the ability "to tolerate the tension" of being open to the experience, and the life story, of another.

To some, the word "tension" may seem inappropriate or even harsh. Nevertheless, I believe it is an accurate description of the experience when one truly listens to the depth of concern in another person. Tension will never be experienced if the conversation remains on the surface and never reaches any depth—the camera looks both ways. However, at its depth, a visit to a young man with cancer who has no hope of going home again to be with his three-year-old son is an experience that will certainly and appropriately evoke tension and cause pain for a pastoral visitor.

In the same way, trying to comfort a mother for the death of her child who is the victim of a drunk driver is an experience that, at its depth, must evoke tension and rip through the soul of any human being. At the depth of empathy, tension and harshness are unavoidable. Being present emotionally, intellectually, and spiritually at these sacred moments can certainly cause tension in a visitor. It is crucial that the visitor be aware of his or her own feelings and of the tensions they bring. Only then will the pastoral visitor be able to attend to himself or herself in order to be present and attend to the person in need.

Because empathy has a cognitive dimension, it requires being open to the point of view of the other person. When that point of view is different from your own, it will likely create a tension on the cognitive level. To "tolerate" this tension requires that you not only listen to the different point of view but also that you be honestly open to it and let the other person know that you understand it. The cognitive aspect of empathy, which involves the ability to take the point of view of another person or "to walk in his shoes," is a difficult but indispensable part of pastoral visitation.

Because empathy also has an affective dimension, it requires us to be open to the emotional experience of the other person. When that emotional experience is different from your own, it will likely create a tension on the affective level. To "tolerate" this tension requires that you make a serious effort to enter the emotional space of the other but also that you accept it "as if" it were your own. The affective aspect of empathy, which involves the ability to be sensitive to the feelings of another and to share in those feelings, is a difficult but indispensable part of pastoral visitation.

Because empathy has these two difficult and indispensable dimensions, the cognitive and the affective, it is not easily achieved. To be successful with empathy, the visitor must attempt "to enter the world" of another person and not only understand what is going on there but also feel what it is like to be there. This is no small feat, and the pastoral visitor must be willing to constantly work on it. Whenever a visitor hears herself saying "I know what you are feeling" or "I know what you are thinking," a red flag should go up in the visitor's mental process. We never know what another is feeling or thinking unless we ask the other. For example, if you are visiting a family that has just learned that their five-year-old son has a life-threatening ill-ness, and if you happen yourself to be the parent of a five-year-old child, you will immediately know on the cognitive level what the news would mean for you. Without asking, you really do not know what it means to the parents receiving this news. We can use our own feelings to help us begin to be present to the situation, but an empathic response will require putting our own feelings aside in order to get in touch with the feelings of the parents before us. It also requires that we put on hold how we might think about the situ-ation, in order to be open to the perspective of this family.

Although, as a pastoral visitor, you are asked to enter the world of another person, you are not required to give up the reality of your own world. You are not asked to give up your own point of view or your own feelings. In some way or other, though, you need to strad-dle the two worlds. By definition, empathy involves the effort to experience both worlds at once and to tolerate the tension that results.

During the pastoral visit, the minister must try to understand the incongruities of the situation and share the emotional content of it while at the same time remaining a differentiated person. It is this twofold combination that makes empathic presence difficult and makes it effective. So it's important for the pastoral visitor to know what it means to "be differentiated" and to be able to do it.

What does it mean to be a differentiated person? David Schnarch states that "differentiation is the ability to maintain your sense of self when you are emotionally and/or physically close to others, espe-cially as they become increasingly important to you." In other words, it is the ability to stay connected with another person without being consumed by that person. If we return to the parents with the five-year-old sick child, your differentiated self will enable you to be pres-ent, feel deeply, and understand their position but not take on the case emotionally as if it were your child.

Differentiation, then, is the ability to establish one's own bound-aries. When visiting several people who are in extreme suffering from sickness or distress, pastoral visitors often find that their own bound-aries become fused with those of the person in need. They cannot always distinguish between their own anxieties and feelings and the anxieties and feelings of the people they visit. Fusion is always undesirable and is especially harmful when, because of it, pastoral visitors are not able to get on well with their own regular lives. The matter of differentiation has serious implications not only for the relationship during the visit but also for the healthy transition to life after the visit.

The Skills of Empathy

To be present to another person in an empathic way means much more than to be in the same place with another person. Central to the practice of empathy in pastoral visitation is the art of an active "listening presence." Empathy, you will recall, involves truly listening to another person and being present to that person in genuine encounter. As with all art, the art of empathy moves toward better performance through the development of skills.

The skills of empathy can be described according to the various ways in which the visitor is able to turn his or her attention to the other person so that it will be on all levels attending to that person: physically, mentally, emotionally, and spiritually. From a pastoral point of view, attending to another person in this way through an active "listening presence" and a "genuine encounter" is an expression not only of pastoral concern for the person you are visiting but also of the deepest respect. Moreover, it is an experience that happens through a mutual exchange of respect by the participants.

Attending physically, of course, means the pastoral visitor and the other person must be in the same place. Additionally, they need to "center," that is, to acknowledge to themselves what is going on in their own lives and to be aware of their own inner lives, their minds and spirit. They must discover if there is anything present that might hinder the process of being actively present to each other. Finding a gentle, silent space in the mind and soul in order to offer gracious openness to the other is an essential condition of attending physically in the skill of empathy. If, after some reflection, you discover that you can not be attending physically, it is advisable to put off the visit to another time.

Attending mentally requires the visitor to discard the distractions of the mind that do not pertain to or assist attention in pastoral visiting. It enables the visitor to enter into the mind-set of the other, so to speak, and to gain a better understanding of his or her point of view. In many cases, concentration on the present will be necessary for the pastoral visitor so as not to be misled by personal concerns or by extraneous details introduced in the dialogue.

Attending emotionally means the ability to be open to the story of the "wounded storyteller" while remaining open to your own story of a "wounded healer." After receiving the diagnosis of an incurable disease, patients are often psychologically traumatized. The body may feel out of control and foreign to the psyche. It is important for the pastoral minister to be in touch with that psychological experience as much as possible as it is communicated by the other person. The visitor's role is to create an atmosphere of acceptance and safety so the traumatic experience can be processed and, with time, integrated into the life of the patient. The ability of the visitor to be truly present to the patient and to hear the disappointment, the frustration, the anger with God expressed in the meeting is truly a gift for the patient.

Attending spiritually means allowing the other person to be who he or she is spiritually without personal prejudice on the part of the visitor. The visitor must be unequivocally accepting of the spiritual sensibilities of the other person. An inappropriate or an inopportune intrusion of the values and beliefs of the visitor into the meeting may become an obstacle to the free expression of the values and beliefs of the person in need. For example, the visitor might feel that the Rosary or a scripture reading would provide healing support in facing the painful reality of a recent diagnosis, but the patient might be very angry with God at this moment, so silent attentiveness may be the best spiritual response. Open discussion and direct inquiry into the patient's spiritual needs can be very therapeutic. In the midst of a traumatic experience or a debilitating illness, quite understandably the patient may at the moment doubt or reject what he or she previously held with faith, clarity, and assurance. Without making assumptions of any kind, the pastoral minister can take the first step in helping the patient discuss what is actually going on in his or her spiritual life. The patient is in charge of this journey and is entitled to take the lead. The visitor is an invited guest, privileged to walk with the patient while trying to attend to his or her needs.

Preparation for the Pastoral Visit

Personal relationship, which is the essence of life and the core of pastoral visitation, most importantly requires many things, among which are notably gentleness, compassion, and empathy with oneself and with the other person. If a meaningful interpersonal exchange is to take place, empathy must work both ways. It is important for the pastoral minister to know his or her capacity at the present time for moving into the world of another, of walking in the shoes of another, while at the same time respecting his or her own vulnerability.

Before each visit and in a spirit of respect, the pastoral visitor must take time to reflect on his or her own emotional and mental experience at the moment. Some days, our hearts and heads are so filled with our own stress and worry that we may not be available to listen to the story of anyone else, especially someone in deep pain. This particular time may or may not be the right time for the visit.

Before each visit, and in a spirit of devotion, the pastoral minister must take time to pray for himself or herself and for the other person. To prepare your own heart and soul to be open to the meeting with the heart and soul of another human being is a work of spiritual grace and humility. Martin Buber described the mysterious nature of this special kind of meeting when he said that "in every true meeting of the I and thou, other is Thou." In his way, Buber was reflecting on what can be recognized theologically as the holiness in unselfish human love and caring. For the Christian pastoral visitor, the experience will be recognized as the presence of God, the incarnational blessing lived in that special moment of grace.

Assessment of the Pastoral Visit

It is important for the pastoral minister to have an awareness of his or her own personal abilities and capabilities that will be employed in the visitation. In order for this to happen, it is necessary to be in touch with one's self-esteem and to be comfortable with it. While visiting is often rewarding and gratifying, it can sometimes also be unsatisfying and difficult. When things don't go well or you don't say the right words at the right time, you can easily become discouraged unless you keep in mind the ordinary limitations to be expected by the very nature of the visit.

Visiting another person is developing a relationship with that person and, as in all relationships, the process takes time. Learning how to visit requires the development of skills and, like all skills, these skills require experience. Should the tensions of active listening and the stress of empathic presence become burdensome for the pastoral visitor, they need to be relieved. It is helpful, for both experienced and inexperienced pastoral visitor, to meet with a supervisor or an advisor of some kind in order to process the dynamics of the visit. Group support and group supervision are extremely valuable and highly recommended for helping the visitor to grow and develop the self-empathy necessary for fruitful ministry.

Purpose in the Pastoral Visit

In addition to being respectful and spiritual, a pastoral visitation must also be intentional, that is, the pastoral visitor must have clear purpose in mind and that purpose must inform the encounter. This is in distinct contrast to the social visit that can shift or change with no loss to the efficacy of the visit. Visiting the sick, the suffering, and the homebound for the sake of pastoral ministry requires certain virtues, among which are humility, compassion, hospitality, and gratitude.

Without the virtues grounded in grace, the pastoral visit is not truly pastoral. In his rules for Christian living, St. Paul offers this ideal of relationship that might easily serve as a motto for the pastoral visitor, "Be happy with those who are happy, weep with those who weep . . . Have the same concern for everyone" (Romans 12:15–16). In this spirit of Christian relationship, the visitor can approach the home of the sick person or the room in the hospital as "sacred ground" and walk humbly in the presence of God. In the spirit of

Christian faith, the visitor and the sick person within the mystery of empathic encounter can recognize the face of Christ in each other and be grateful for consolation and healing in the light of grace.

Hospitality in the Pastoral Visit

David Augsburger offers a reflection on the notion of hospitality that, to my mind, accurately describes the situation in a pastoral visitation. It is a simple reminder that the patient is the host and the pastoral visitor is the guest. And so it follows that "it is the host, not the guest, who owns the life story and the human experiences that are shared." At the center of the sacred space is the "wounded storyteller." Not the guest but the host/hostess belongs in the center space. The visit takes place on the "sacred ground" of the recipient's space at a time when that personal space is filled with the mystery of suffering or distress.

The pastoral visitor is welcomed into the story not merely of the one person being encountered but also of the family, the community, and the church to which he or she belongs. Since the visitor enters by invitation and not by intrusion, honoring the rules of the house and respecting the religious and moral values cherished there are serious matters of courtesy and respect. As a visitor with pastoral purpose, the minister avoids the role of invader or spy and conscientiously respects the etiquette, rituals, secrets, and privacy of the family into which he or she has been welcomed as an honorary, though temporary, member.

Just as the rule of hospitality obliges the host always to be gracious to the guest, so the same rule of hospitality obliges the guest never to forget whose house it is. It would be an egregious discourtesy for the guest to rearrange the furniture either physically or symbolically. The very disposition to rearrange furniture would indicate a failure in prayerful preparation to enter into that place in the spirit of service for the other, which is indispensable in pastoral ministry: "We must empty ourselves to prepare to be a guest, to be truly present in another's world, to enter it sensitively, caringly, humbly, as guests. For so we are," says David Augsburger.

On the deeper level of mystical meaning, the pastoral visitor and the person in need are both guests in a house of blessing. They are both guests on "sacred ground," which any place becomes because of divine presence through grace. If it is truly "sacred ground" in that sense, then for both of them it is not a matter of hospitality and the courtesy of host and guest that embrace them in the visit, but a solemn obligation of reverence toward each other and toward God in this healing encounter. The blessing experienced in the act of ministry is fulfillment of the prayer, fervently spoken by the psalmist and etched deeply in our human desire, for a divine union in love. It is a prayer that the pastoral minister might wish to be the fulfillment of every ministry of visitation to the sick and to the bereaved:

> I have asked the Lord for one thing
> one thing only do I want:
> to live in the Lord's house all my life,
> to marvel at his goodness,
> and to ask for his guidance. (Psalm 27:4)

As pilgrims on the journey of life, we have no real home for the spirit. The fragile dwellings of earth pass away; we have only the spiritual lodgings of the heart. These are the dwelling place of love and charity that never passes away and in which God forever dwells.

References

Augsburger, David (1994). "Diversity and Variety: Creativity and Spirituality or Competition and Conflict?" Presented at NOCERCC 21st Annual Convention, February 7–10, 1994. San Diego, California.

Buber, M. (1957). *I and Thou*. Translated by R. G. Smith. New York: Charles Scribner's Sons. (1970 edition translated by W. Kaufmann. New York: Scribner).

Friedman, Edwin H. (1985). *Generation to Generation*. New York: The Guilford Press.

Musgrave, Beverly Anne (in press). "Empathy: The Heart of Intimacy." In *Pastoral Counseling in Context: Questions of Gender, Value & Culture*. The Society for Pastoral Counseling Research.

The New Jerusalem Bible (1985). New York: Doubleday.

Patterson, Freeman (1996). *A Photographer's Life: Shadow Light*. Toronto: HarperCollins Publishers.

Schnarch, David (1997). *Passionate Marriage*. New York: Henry Holt & Company.

For Further Reading

Bohart, Arthur C., & Greenberg, L. S., eds. (1997). *Empathy Reconsidered*. Washington, D.C.: American Psychological Association.

Ciaramicoli, A. P., & Ketcham, K. (1997). *The Power of Empathy*. New York: Penguin Group.

Goldstein, A., & Michaels, Gerald Y. (1985). *Empathy, Development, Training and Consequences*. Hillsdale, N.J.: Lawrence Erlbaum Associates.

Hart, Thomas N. (1980). *The Art of Christian Listening*. Mahwah, N.J.: Paulist Press.

Hill, Clare E., & O'Brien, Karen M. (1999). *Helping Skills*. Washington, D.C.: American Psychological Association.

Jacobs, Michael (1985). *Swift to Hear: Facilitating Skills in Listening and Responding*. London: SPCK.

Lichtenber, J., Bornstein, M., Silver, D., eds. (1984). *Empathy I & II*. Hillsdale, N.J.: Lawrence Erlbaum Associates.

Nichols, Michael P. (1995). *The Lost Art of Listening*. New York: The Guilford Press.

Tournier, Paul (1987). *A Listening Ear*. Minneapolis: Augsburg Press.

Visiting Those Who Mourn

Sarah L. Fogg

Receiving emotional and spiritual care in the midst of loss is one of the deepest needs of any human being. Offering this support is one of the greatest acts of loving kindness, because the exchange always occurs on uncomfortable, often painful terrain. Preparing yourself to offer care to a person who is suffering is not an easy task. First, you must be willing to look at your own experiences of loss and then share your feelings about loss with another person. (See the preparation exercises at the end of this chapter.) You are offering yourself as *a partner* in healing: someone who has also been wounded by loss but is able to withstand the difficulties of being present to another who is going through grief right now. You do *not* come as one who knows how to fix deep grief with a few well-chosen words and techniques. To do so would be to betray the truth: grieving is as much a spiritual task as an emotional task. Much of it is divine work, accomplished with great effort and, when effective, with God's help.

As you listen to someone talk about personal grief, you will experience "sympathetic" feelings of anxiety and emotional pain. Unless you are aware that this happens and can identify your feelings, your visit will be compromised. You may confuse your own feelings for those of the grieving person and focus on them instead. Also, unacknowledged anxieties may be so overpowering that you unconsciously change the conversation to a less painful subject.

Everyone wounded by loss is "wired" for healing. That is, we all have an emotional or spiritual pathway designed to return us to wholeness. To be an effective visitor, you need to know how this wiring works for recovery. It will prepare you to recognize where someone may be stuck and need your assistance to move into the next phase. It will also help you see if an important step has been missed and needs to be explored.

Psychologists studying loss and bereavement have identified stages of psychological adjustment or adaptation that lead to recovery or acceptance. Elisabeth Kubler-Ross described a five-step process of mourning—denial, anger, bargaining, preparatory depression, and acceptance—experienced by the terminally ill. Other psychologists have developed multi-stage models of grieving for survivors of loss. One of the most helpful is that of Erich Neumann, described below. Judith Savage used this model to further develop insights into the particularly sensitive area of grieving miscarriage. The Neumann model will serve as our psychological base.

We will draw upon two well-known stories of the Bible, for we serve as visitors because of our religious commitment to be caring neighbors to those in need. The story of Job, in the Hebrew scriptures, and Jesus' birth and death, as portrayed by Luke in the Christian scriptures, represent, in sacred narrative, how to heal through grieving. These biblical stories and the Neumann psychological model provide the tools you will need to visit those suffering the grief of loss.

Finally, the loss of a child during pregnancy will serve as a stereotype for all grief and loss. Until recently, religious, social, and medical institutions were silent about pregnancy loss. It was generally treated as insignificant, and mourners were provided no grief support through ritual, custom, or protocol. Rather than misunderstanding or minimizing the grief of would-be parents, it is far more likely that these institutions found pregnancy loss "too hot to handle" and retreated into unconscious denial. No event has more potential to cause a crisis of meaning than the death of a loved one, but in pregnancy loss, an even greater crisis of meaning is likely to occur. Assistance from caregivers is especially needed, for, in this instance, birth and death are one. In spiritual terms, the mourner is challenged with making sense of the two greatest mysteries of life—birth and death—simultaneously. Psychologically, the mourner must attach and detach at the same time. In pregnancy loss, connection to the loved one has been made from hopes, plans, and dreams for the future. These must be consciously claimed at the very moment death has torn them away. Such pain tempts the mourner to deny what was hoped for, but doing so would disconnect him or her from the healing process. The "wiring" that leads to recovery requires that all the parts, or stages, of grief be connected. The dramatic and extra-sensitive nature of pregnancy loss will heighten your understanding of each stage of grief for all loss.

Neumann's five-part psychological model appears below. The stories of Job and Jesus are referenced above it. I have arranged Neumann's model in an inverted triangle to suggest the emotional descent triggered by loss and the eventual ascent to healing. Neumann views his entire model as a ritual that he describes as an archetype of the way toward healing. I have inserted "ritual" as a particular ceremony and have placed it near the lowest point of the model. Ritual as ceremony is typically employed closely following the death of a loved one. However, it can be used at any time, for its function is to direct mourners toward recovery and healing. Composed of the structural elements of religion (music, prayer, ceremony, rite, narrative, gathered and loving community, etc.), ritual works to impart new life to the survivors of serious loss.

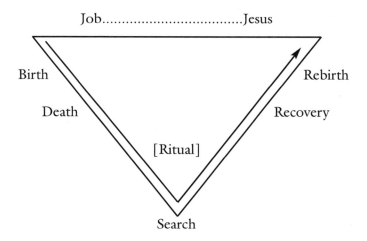

Stage One: Birth/Attaching

It is not easy to help mourners with the first stage of grieving. They must remember and claim what they have lost. They need to attach to the memories of the one they loved and to everything that bound them together. You can help them do that by listening and by encouraging them to talk as much as they can. Since you cannot replace what or whom they have lost, you may experience feelings of helplessness. Be careful to not let your feelings push the mourners away from the important work of remembrance. It is the first connection in the healing "wiring" that must be made.

Spending time with a mourner in stage one is particularly difficult in pregnancy loss. The urge to give false reassurances is very strong. The fact that there was little or no bonding outside the womb with one who could be seen and touched may deceive you into thinking there is nothing to remember. But there were hopes, plans, and dreams; these were lost. If they are not claimed, or if they are denied, grieving will be "short-circuited." Instead of being erased, grief will erupt in disguised forms. Unacknowledged, it will remain to fester, unhealed.

It is unlikely that anyone would say to a grieving parent whose six-year-old child has died, "Oh well, you can have another child," or "How fortunate that it wasn't your ten-year-old child whom you've known and loved a lot longer." In pregnancy loss, well-intentioned family members, medical staff, even clergy, may try to minimize what has happened with comments such as these. Intending to save parents from present emotional pain, the well-wisher stands unwittingly in the way of genuine healing. Healing always begins with claiming the dream, acknowledging the great hope and the relationship that already existed between the would-be parents and the unborn child. Betty, who miscarried in the third month of her first pregnancy, is an example of someone who was deprived of that experience. Her doctor told her not to think or worry about the miscarriage. He was sure she could get pregnant again.

"I wasn't attached to the child, so I didn't have a bond," she says now, with tears in her eyes. "I miscarried on a Friday. I didn't even miss work. It was simple in that sense. What I remember most was that it was quick and easy. The doctor met me at his office right away. I wasn't in a lot of pain. I thought of it in medical terms: an incomplete pregnancy. That's how it was diagnosed. I was very matter-of-fact about it; not cold, but without real emotions. That's the way I felt about it. It was an unhappy experience, but not a real life-changing one. Not like Judy's accident." (She is referring to a serious accident involving the daughter she later had; the family received good pastoral care and grew spiritually through the frightening ordeal.)

Competing feelings in the first stage of grief can also make it difficult to take the first step toward healing. These feelings create an opposing tension: joy versus fear and doubt. The joy of affirming the hopes and dreams already attached to the lost child is scary: Will claiming them deepen the pain of loss? Will this happen again? Would it be better to shield oneself against hopes and dreams until there is certainty?

In our two biblical narratives, Job, a father, and Mary, a mother, exhibit this same tension: The mere thought of loss dampens joy. Amidst idyllic harmony, and without the slightest inkling of trouble regarding his children, Job ritually purifies them through animal sacrifice on a regular basis—just in case. Mary, who responded with joy to the angel's announcement that she would be the mother of Jesus, hears the shepherds marveling at what they too had heard about her baby from the angels. But Mary "kept all these things, pondering them in her heart."

The mourner's task in the first stage of grief is to own the dreams, plans, and hopes for the child. To do it in the face of death is challenging. Psychologically, the mourner must firmly attach herself to what has been lost. Your task as visitor is twofold. First, as will be true for each stage of grieving, you must show care and concern without advising, critiquing, or minimizing. Second, you must enable the grieving survivor to affirm her hopes and dreams. Listen carefully to see where the mourner is emotionally. She may be already focusing on the second step of grieving, on the actual death—on the ordeal of the miscarriage or stillbirth—how it happened, what it was like. But somewhere, early on, if she does not describe her dashed hopes and dreams, you can help by making comments like, "You must have had great plans..." or "There were so many things you had hoped to do with your child."

Remembering the lost one in the presence of a sympathetic listener is a necessary step for all those who grieve. The mourner may idealize the deceased person or express feelings of guilt that something was left undone or that harsh words that cannot be taken back were spoken. Remember, you are not to argue or give false assurances. You are to listen and to encourage the mourner to go deeper into remembrance. You might say, "You really loved so-and-so deeply," or ask, "What do you wish you had said or done?"

Stage Two: Death/Detaching

In the second stage of grieving pregnancy loss, the tension results not from competing feelings but from the lack of space or time between birth and death. In all other deaths, the mourner has had living time with the departed. With birth and death occurring simultaneously in pregnancy loss, there is no "space," no place to anchor oneself emotionally. The mourner's task in stage two is to acknowledge the loss of her dream, of her plans and hopes for the child. You, as a visitor, must continue to show care and support for the mourner, and you must enable her to acknowledge that the hoped-for child is dead.

While it is painful to talk about the hopes and dreams one had in the face of death, it is just as difficult for many to speak of a loved one as dead. It is also a challenge for you, the visitor, to listen to such talk, for it arouses your own anxieties about death. But you are present to help the mourner successfully navigate the sacred path of grieving. If the survivor is already able to talk about the death, how it happened, how she felt, who was present, etc., your job is to listen and encourage the telling of the story. If she is avoiding the subject, you can help by making comments like, "I am so sorry for your loss" or "What did you think/feel when you first realized this was happening?"

In the Bible, Luke frames this part of Jesus' story dramatically. He describes Mary standing with friends, watching the cruel, painful death of her son. The writer of Job heightens the drama of this stage of grieving by piling one calamity upon the next until only one servant is left to run and inform Job of his latest loss. Finally, Job hears that the worst has happened. Not only has he lost all of his possessions, he has also lost all of his children to tragic death.

In a case of pregnancy loss, Barbara was also overwhelmed by losing one thing after another: "I was settled into having the baby. It had been hard. I was a single person, and when I confronted the father, he rejected me and said the baby wasn't his! That really hurt. And my mother. She was always saying she was mourning for me and that I had broken my father's heart. And then it happened, while we were at my sister's for the holidays. I felt kind of funny because I was looking forward to having the baby. Here I had fought all those fights, and then it was taken away from me, and I realized I really wanted it. That was the third rejection I felt. Boom, boom, boom."

Confronted with emotional and spiritual pain like Barbara's, family members or hospital staff may offer to relieve the mourner from dealing with painful tasks—making decisions about burial or cremation, choosing a ritual for a funeral or blessing, etc. Even adults facing their own deaths may leave instructions for no funerals or memorial services in an attempt to lessen the sadness and pain of their survivors. Such well-intentioned, but uninformed, gestures can deprive mourners of the very thing that can move them toward healing: ritual.

Ritual's ultimate purpose is transformation. Its more immediate purpose is simply to point to the mourner's hoped-for transformation or recovery. For most mourners, the mysteries, tensions, and contradictions of loss are too great in the first few days surrounding the death of a loved one even for comprehension, let alone transformation. Ritual provides a spiritual place worthy of holding brokenness until grief works its way through to wholeness. The story of Joseph of Arimathea tenderly burying the body of Jesus in a beautiful, special place is instructive. In grief, one needs to do something for the dead and for oneself. Ritual is a sacred exchange that recognizes and honors deep loss. It also helps make room in the heart for the continuing work of grief.

Some hospitals have established protocols that support the grieving parents of pregnancy loss and assist them in moving into the first two grief stages. Nurses are trained to listen to patients as they talk about the emotional reactions to their loss. Nurses take color photos of the baby, make foot or hand print records, and encourage the parents to see and hold the baby—even to name it. Hospital chaplains assist in listening to parents, offer rituals of blessing or naming, and help the parents deal with cremation and burial arrangements. All of this helps the survivors acknowledge their loss and begin the psychological process of detaching from what is no longer possible. Hospital staffs have discovered a twofold result. For the parents, grieving appropriately helps to restore a healthy capacity for parenting a future child. Staff members who learn to tolerate their patients' intense emotions receive the personal satisfaction of coping better with their own feelings as well as the lasting gratitude of the bereaved parents.

Stage Three: The Search/Attempting to Fill the Void

The third stage of grieving is usually the longest and the most lonely. Friends and family who make special efforts to be present and comforting to survivors in the beginning of their loss or at the funeral are often less present and supportive during this period. As a visitor, you can be a welcome presence to mourners, for this is usually when they feel—and are—most alone and abandoned. The bereaved must go through everything, over and over, in an attempt to discover how this could have happened, who is responsible, and why it happened. Psychologically, mourners are attempting to fill the void left by the loss of their loved one. A woman who miscarries may reason that if a cause can be identified, perhaps such a thing can be prevented from ever happening again; it can be "put right." The search continues until no more energy is left to continue. This is precisely the mourners' task in stage three and it makes it difficult for others to "walk with them."

To those who are not grieving, this stage appears fruitless, even counterproductive, for it seems only to make the survivors sadder, more depressed, and unable to turn their attention to happier, more life-oriented alternatives. You are also likely to feel uneasy. Monitor your emotions carefully. Refrain from giving advice or quick solutions. Instead, listen with compassion as those whom you visit explore this painful territory, for there are no short-cuts through it.

What are the emotions of the mourner at this stage of grief? While loneliness, abandonment, and emptiness are typical, the one feeling shared by almost everyone is guilt. Neils Lauerseiv, M.D., Ph.D., a professor of obstetrics and gynecology at New York Medical College, writing of pregnancy loss says that "a woman's first reaction is almost always an attempt to find guilt in herself. It's hard to believe that something that happened inside your own body was not, in some way, your fault. Women who miscarry often pick over everything they've done, even felt and thought—like dogged prosecutors hunting for enough evidence to convict."

Rhonda remembers her guilt and how it was nurtured by comments made by her family that were meant to be helpful: "I did feel guilty. What caused it? I tried to figure out what I did. Maybe I lifted too much. I remember my family always saying, 'You're lifting too much. Take it easy.'"

Anger is also quick to erupt in stage three, as in stage two, especially anger directed at others. Job was angry at the wicked who prospered while he suffered. Tanya shared Job's feelings: "It was devastating. I was in a deep depression. I couldn't think of anything else. I was angry with God: 'Why can't I have a baby?' I couldn't look at anyone who was pregnant. I understood why there are baby snatchers."

Spiritually, the search of stage three is an attempt to fill the void with meaning, to find an answer to the question, "Why did this happen?" Pregnancy loss is particularly poignant, for an innocent child has been lost. For a religious person, this can pose a terrible spiritual crisis. If God is all-powerful and all-loving, why would God allow the death of an innocent? This question is at the heart of Job's suffering. It is also present in Jesus' crucifixion. Why would a father allow his son to die such a cruel death? Many pastoral visitors cannot bear the suffering or anger some mourners experience as they struggle with their faith in the midst of deep loss. Job's friends couldn't, and criticized him for questioning God. You, too, may find this difficult. If you have worked through a spiritual crisis of your own, you may be tempted to offer it to the one grieving now. But each of us must find our own way through grief. There are no substitutes, however lovingly given. Your ministry is one of partnership. You are present to care for and support the one who mourns now and to watch and wait as the sacred task of mourning moves toward healing and recovery.

To the human eye, nothing happens in the third stage of mourning. But it is not so. Emptiness is not just a feeling during the search; it is the goal. Until the strong emotions focused "backward" upon loss are totally spent, it is impossible to move forward toward recovery. Paradoxically, by listening to and supporting the bereaved, without attempting to hurry them through, you can be instrumental in helping them move through this stage more quickly.

Stage Four: Recovery/Remembering and Envisioning

Almost always, in stage three, the mourner has made a vow to remember, to never forget the one who was lost. In stage four, the emphasis subtly shifts from past to future. No longer able to focus on the details of the loss, the mourner finds herself envisioning what the child would have been like, how he or she would have looked at different ages, what paths in life the child might have taken. Linda put it this way: "Part of my own grieving was saying goodbye. I tried to imagine what the child might have looked like. I had a funny feeling that if it had come to term, it would have been a boy, but it was just an odd thing, intuition. I remember imagining what that would be like, to have a baby boy."

Eventually, as the mourner continues to envision and "remember" forward, an inner image of the child is born. As it takes root, develops, and becomes more defined, the energy that was impelling the searching stage of mourning abates and the parent begins to trust again in the eternal bond of attachment. Barbara remembers that during her grieving, she experienced this transition: "At the beginning, I visualized what could have been. How would it have turned out if the baby had lived? I watched infants and said, 'Why not me?' It got replaced gradually. It became self-acceptance of who

I am. The visualization, I gave it up, although it still lingers on around July [the baby's due date]."

The forward movement of stage four includes a subtle transformation that results in a remembered image of the child that is different from previous images. Often people shrink back from viewing the deceased, fearful that they will remember them always in that death pose. Such is not the case for those who keep on the sacred path of mourning, who search as long as they can until, exhausted, they cease. We are mysteriously "wired" for renewal and transformation, especially in grief and loss.

One woman experienced it this way: "Not long ago, when my husband and I were telling a friend about our miscarriage, I said the baby was normal size. I remember my surprise when my husband disagreed, and said that the baby was very small, no more than eight inches long. I realized I remembered him quite differently now."

In psychological terms, the transformation of the inner image of the lost child helps loosen the bonds with the actual dead child while preserving the parent's spiritual connection to the child. Both psychology and religion understand recovery as beginning with the bereaved being comforted with a sense of spiritual presence that seems to come from outside them, a presence that springs slowly, yet surely, from the fount of remembrance. Once recognized, it brings the bereaved back to life, not just restored, but ready to be enlarged.

In the stories of Job and Jesus, the survivors discover that their lost relationship has returned in unexpected forms. God finally shows up and talks with Job, not as a courtroom judge but as a tour guide of the universe. Jesus catches up to the two travelers to Emmaus who fail to recognize him as he listens to their tale of disappointment and loss. Then he speaks, taking them back through the scriptures, stirring their memory and their soul's imaginings of the coming glory foretold, "beginning with Moses and all the prophets." Both Job and the travelers experience a breakthrough, which the religious call "revelation." They receive a knowledge and experience a presence different from what they could have thought or imagined from their former theological perspective.

As visitor and partner in the journey toward wholeness, you can play an important role in helping the mourner become aware of the changes occurring in his or her memory and imaginings. You might say, for example, "You seem closer to, and more at peace with, the one you lost as you speak." Don't expect to witness the dramatic, instantaneous change reported in our Bible stories. For most, it is a gradual realization, sometimes marked by survivors' fears that finding peace and joy again are betrayals to the memory of the one who has died. Be patient and kind as you continue to show support in your ministry. Everyone has his or her own special timing.

Stage Five: Rebirth/Embracing the Future

The mourner's task in the final stage of grieving is to experience and recognize the transformation from brokenness to wholeness. The tension present at this stage is between the need to release oneself from the depths of grief and the desire to remember the deceased forever. Your role as visitor is, as always, to show care and support for the mourner and to be witness to his or her joy and return to wholeness.

Rebirth is usually expressed in terms of a gift. Recovered mourners feel enlarged by some new understanding or breakthrough that comes from outside them that can be generously shared. The writer of Job expresses it as the return of all of Job's possessions, doubled. He lives twice as long as his age at the time of the tragedy and is blessed by more children. He asks God to forgive his three advice-giving friends. Jesus' formerly frightened and confused disciples receive the Holy Spirit and become confident and powerful, able to speak their newfound word in foreign languages and preach the "Good News" to others.

Rhonda experienced it as a new way of seeing: "I learned not to take life so lightly—or to take it so heavily. Laugh a little more. Enjoy life. Live! It wasn't what I didn't have; it was what I did have. I began to see life from a whole different perspective."

Gift is given in the context of community. Job's story ends with his entire clan surrounding him. Jesus' disciples find new and powerful community, first in Jerusalem, and then far beyond in the enlivened, growing community of Christians.

Barbara experienced this with her father: "The trauma broke a barrier between me and my father. We became very close. My father started the conversation. In talking, I was no longer the little girl; I was the adult. It was acceptance of a different kind."

Nancy recognized how her experience connected her more closely to others experiencing loss: "It makes me far more sensitive to other people when I hear about their losses. It's a very traumatic thing. I think people who have not experienced it don't understand. Some people think if you've never had something, you can't lose it. But losing a child in pregnancy is a real loss."

Lucy said: "When someone else loses a child, I feel a lot more sympathy. A friend of mine once asked me what to do for a friend who had just had a Down-syndrome baby. I told her, 'You just be there for her and tell her, "I am your friend. If you want to talk about it, I will listen."' You don't need somebody talking at you. You need someone listening to you."

As these brief testimonies reveal, survivors of grief who make their way through deep loss find unexpected strength, knowledge of themselves, and a deeper connection with humanity. They also experience the joy and awe that comes with such revelation. It is felt in the resurgence of trust, hope, the promise of the future, openness to life—all the childlike qualities that disappear in the grief of miscarriage, indeed, in the grief of all loss. When they return, as they do for all who stay on the sacred path of mourning, they are experienced as rebirth and the beginning of new, expanded life.

Conclusion

Every human being is "wired" to be restored to wholeness. The task is made lighter and easier when there are others along the path of mourning who can be present and supportive. There are, however, some times when previous losses and circumstances have seriously compromised a mourner's natural ability to move toward healing. If you suspect that the person whom you are visiting needs more help than you can provide, you should share your concerns with your supervisor or clergy person.

In most cases, your care and support will be exactly what is needed by a survivor of loss, and you have much to offer. You have a particular task in each of the five stages of grieving. And you have a constant task throughout: to always show your care and concern to the one who mourns. You do so by being present and by listening—even to what you may have heard before. It is also important to continuously monitor your own emotions, especially when you feel the urge to explain, give advice, or hurry the mourner along because you are uncomfortable with the feelings his or her sadness or anger is evoking in you. After a while you will notice that your ability to be present and listen encourages the mourner to uncover deeper emotions and concerns. Your affirmation and presence will often have the effect of enabling mourners to access what they need from their own religious or spiritual resources. This will be a gift to you. You will see what you never could have imagined yourself. It will delight you and make you glad that you have been privileged to be part of God's divine work: restoring the brokenhearted to wholeness.

For Further Reading

Furman, E. P. (1978). "The Death of a Newborn: Care of the Parents." *Birth and Family Journal, 5,* 214–218.

Kohn, Ingrid, & Moffitt, Perry-Lynn (1992). *A Silent Sorrow: Pregnancy Loss.* New York: Delacorte Press.

Kubler-Ross, E. (1969). *On Death and Dying.* New York: Macmillan.

Neumann, E. (1970). *The Origins and History of Consciousness.* Princeton: Princeton University Press.

Pizer, Hank, & Palinski, Christine O'Brien (1980). *Coping with a Miscarriage.* New York: New American Library.

Savage, Judith A. (1989). *Mourning Unlived Lives: A Psychological Study of Childbearing Loss.* Wilmette, Illinois: Chiron Press.

Weller, Sheila (1988). "Miscarriage: Understanding the Special Grief Women Feel." *Glamour,* November, 88, 93, 95–96, 102.

APPENDIX

Preparation Exercises

A shared experience of loss.

Choose a partner, preferably someone who is also training to be a visitor to those experiencing grief. Identify a loss (of a loved one or of something cherished—a pet, a job, a former state of health, etc.) that you will talk about with your listening partner. Begin by describing why and how you loved whom or what you once had. Provide some details. Next, tell how the loss occurred, where you were at the time, what your feelings were, and the facts of what happened. Talk about what you did and how you felt as you grieved the loss.

What was the hardest part?

What helped you? What did not help you?

How long did it take for you to begin to come out of your grief?

What signs do you remember?

Looking back on the experience now, what has changed in you as a result of going through this loss and its grief?

Once you have finished, reverse roles. Following the steps in the exercise above, listen to your partner describe an experience of loss and grief.

A guided meditation

If it is not possible to find a partner for the first exercise, you may go through it individually, using the suggestions in the partner exercise above as a guided meditation. You will find it more helpful to respond out loud or to write down your thoughts as you go through the exercise on your own.

Practice Exercises for the Five Stages of Grief

Although each visit and each person visited will be unique, the following exercises are offered to give you practice in responding as a caring listener who is aware of the five stages of grief. You will not always go through them in the same exact order, nor will the mourner. For example, someone in stage three may need to go back to stage one or two in order to continue or to complete that stage.

1. Birth (attaching)

You are visiting a young woman who has just returned home from the hospital where she had a pregnancy loss.

Visitor: Hello, Jeanne. I am so glad to be able to visit with you for a few minutes this afternoon. It sounds like you've been through a difficult time.

Jeanne: Yes, it wasn't easy. I'm trying to be strong. I want to put it all behind me. Nothing can be done about it, so there's no use dwelling on it. The doctor told us we could start trying again very soon.

Visitor: *Response #1.* That's wonderful. But you really can't put it behind you just yet. You need to grieve for what was lost.

   Response #2. That's wonderful. How many children do you want to have?

   Response #3. That's wonderful. But it must be hard to lose what you wanted so much.

Discussion: All three responses are good in affirming the hopes of the mourner. Response #1, though true, argues with the mourner. Response #2 ignores the present sadness and focuses on the future, which does not help the mourner explore the early stages of grief. Response #3 offers the mourner an opportunity to talk about what has been lost.

You are visiting an elderly man whose wife died three months ago.

Visitor: Hello, Mr. Johnson. I am so glad to see you and find
                   out how you are doing.
Mr. Johnson: Thank you for coming. It gets mighty lonely around
                   here without Midge this time of evening.
Visitor: *Response #1.* I imagine it does. What are you doing to
                   keep busy?
                   Response #2. I imagine it does. What did you and she
                   used to do this time of evening?
                   Response #3. Before I forget, let me tell you about the
                   church supper we are having next week.
Discussion: Response #2 is the most appropriate, since it offers
                   Mr. Johnson the chance to recall what was lost. The
                   other responses lead him away from stage one.

2. Death (detaching)

*You are visiting a couple who have experienced a pregnancy loss some-
time in the past. They have shown you the nursery and the gifts they
received for the expected child. You notice that they do not speak of the
child as gone.*

Visitor: Both of you are very clear about the hopes you had
                   for Virginia if she had lived.
Parents: Oh yes. Talking about our dreams for her helps us get
                   through all this.
Visitor: *Response #1.* It's good that you have each other to
                   share your thoughts and feelings with.
                   Response #2. It must be difficult to realize she is no
                   longer here. What was the first sign that something
                   was wrong?
                   Response #3. It is so important to count our blessings.
Discussion: Response #2 shows compassion and offers the parents
                   the chance to explore stage two with a sympathetic lis-

tener who is not afraid to hear their sadness. The first response is caring, but does not help them move into the grief stage they may be avoiding. The third response is a platitude. Platitudes usually fall "flat" unless they are expressed by the mourner.

You are visiting someone who was not able to attend the funeral of a parent who died in a distant state.

Visitor:	Hello, Jim. I heard about your father's death and wanted to stop by and see how you were doing.
Jim:	I'm fine. I don't think it has hit me yet, since I wasn't able to go to the funeral. I still think of him as alive, even though I know he isn't.
Visitor:	*Response #1.* That's understandable. How did his death come about?
	Response #2. Oh, don't worry about it. It will hit you soon enough.
	Response #3. Maybe by the time it does sink in, you will be used to the idea and not be so sad.
Discussion:	The first response affirms Jim where he is now and offers him the opportunity to begin exploring stage two. Response #2 offers neither the opportunity to explore stage two nor the presence of the visitor when sadness appears. Response #3 implies that Jim can find healing without facing the facts or going through all five stages of grief.

3. The Search (attempting to fill the void)

You are making yet another visit, several weeks later, to a young woman who has had a pregnancy loss.

Visitor:	Hello, Jeanne. It's good to stop by and see you again. How are you doing?

Jeanne:	Not so well. I keep going over everything that happened, but it doesn't make me feel better. I know people don't want to hear about this anymore, so I don't talk about it very often to anyone.
Visitor:	Please tell me about it. I don't mind listening at all. In fact, that's exactly what I'd like to do.
Jeanne:	I was trying to keep myself healthy, but I wonder if maybe I exercised too much.
Visitor:	*Response: #1.* What makes you think that? *Response #2.* You were trying to do everything you could to ensure a healthy baby. *Response #3.* Don't be so hard on yourself. I'm sure that it wasn't anything you did that caused the miscarriage.
Discussion:	Response #3 argues with the mourner and gives guarantees outside the visitor's power. Response #1 offers Jeanne the chance to explore further. Response #2 offers comfort and affirmation.

You are visiting a single woman who cared for her mother at home for two years before she died.

Visitor:	The last time I was here, you said you just couldn't forgive yourself for going home that night from the hospital because your mother died before you returned in the morning.
Carol:	Yes, I keep thinking about that. I just can't let it go.
Visitor:	Tell me about that night.
Carol:	(Speaks for several minutes, pouring out a lot of guilt.)
Visitor:	*Response #1.* I think you are being too hard on yourself. *Response #2.* What else have you been worrying about? *Response #3.* You've begun to repeat yourself. You need to let go of these worries and move on.
Discussion:	Response #1 argues with Carol, and Response #3 urges her to leave this stage before it is completed. Only Response #2 offers to stay with her as she explores further.

4. Recovery (remembering and envisioning)

You are visiting Jeanne again as she recovers from grieving her child lost in pregnancy.

Visitor: It has been a while since we last spoke of your loss. How are you now?

Jeanne: I think I am a little better, at least on some days. I still cry when I think about what happened, but I notice I am not quite so sad as when you were here the last time.

Visitor: Oh?

Jeanne: Yesterday, I laughed at some jokes with some friends.

Visitor: How was that for you?

Jeanne: I was happy in some ways, but in others I wondered if I am leaving my baby's memory behind.

Visitor: *Response #1.* Well, you do have to move on.

            Response #2. Oh, I am sure you will always remember him.

            Response #3. It isn't always simple moving forward, even when it feels right to do so.

Discussion: Response #1 expresses the frustration or impatience of the visitor. Response #2 is a statement of fact, which includes some comfort. Response #3 mirrors or restates Jeanne's feelings and allows her to continue.

You are paying a return visit to the widower, Mr. Johnson, some months later.

Visitor: I am wondering how you are now that several months have passed since Midge's death.

Mr. Johnson: I'm not sure. Some days I think I'm coming out of it.

Visitor: What do you mean?

Mr. Johnson: For the first time last week I was able to remember her with a smile and not cry when I was telling my neighbor about one of Midge's adventures in the car.

Visitor: *Response #1.* That's wonderful. It sounds like you are
                finding more peace with her death.
                Response #2. What adventure was that?
                Response #3. Did I ever tell you about my wife's death?
Discussion: Response #1 is affirming and offers a reading of Mr.
                Johnson's feelings that he can agree with or deny.
                Response #2 gives him the opportunity to re-live the
                recovery experience. Response #3 serves the visitor's
                needs rather than Mr. Johnson's.

5. Rebirth (embracing the future)

You are visiting the young woman who had a pregnancy loss last year.

Visitor: We haven't met for several months. How are you?
Jeanne: I think I'm fine. In fact, something happened the other
                day that made me feel good. One of my friends had a
                miscarriage and told me about it. I was able to listen to
                her without worrying about my own problems. I didn't
                actually say very much, but she seemed to really appre-
                ciate my being there with her.
Visitor: *Response #1.* How fortunate she was to have you to talk
                with.
                Response #2. I wonder if your own loss has given you a
                special understanding you didn't have before.
Discussion: The first response affirms Jeanne's return to wholeness
                by celebrating with her a recent joy. The second response
                offers her the opportunity to recognize a gift she has
                received from the journey through grief.

You are visiting the man who wasn't able to attend his father's funeral.

Visitor: Hello, Jim. How have you been?
Jim: Oh, hi. I've been wanting to see you to thank you for
                suggesting that I talk with other family members who

were at my father's funeral. My brother and I have been telephoning each other every week for quite a while. We never used to have that much in common. In a strange way, our father's death brought us into closer contact.

Visitor: *Response #1.* I am so pleased to hear about that.

               Response #2. Tell me what that has been like. It sounds wonderful.

Discussion: Both responses are affirming and celebrate the recovered mourner's joy. The second response provides Jim an opportunity to talk further about what has happened.

Presence: An Active Silence

Beverly Anne Musgrave

Introduction

The prologue to the Gospel of John opens with a passage announcing the great mystery of the Incarnation, the central mystery of the Christian religion. Hidden in the language of poetic imagery and buried under the implications of philosophical speculation there appears a message that a person of faith can put simply in a few often repeated words of praise, "Jesus is Lord."

> In the beginning was the Word;
> the Word was with God,
> and the Word was God. (John 1:1–2)

An uncomplicated statement of the mystery can be made in a simple sentence: Jesus is the Word and the Word is God.

From a theological point of view, meanings can be piled upon meanings in order to shape complex explanations about the humanity and the divinity of Jesus of Nazareth who lived and walked the earth in Galilee and Jerusalem two thousand years ago and Jesus, the Word of God, who lived before the beginning of anything and created the earth and the time in which the earth exists. But the meaning is best expressed in the inspired words of the gospel that continue to tell us what we will never understand but is all we will ever know about that great mystery of faith.

The Word became flesh,
he lived among us,
and we saw his glory,
the glory that he has from the Father,
full of grace and truth. (John 1:14)

Christians who are firm in their faith accept that Jesus is truly divine and truly human, and so they accept the mystery of the Incarnation, but often they accept it without reflection on what it means for them as they live our human lives day by day.

Elsewhere, in the Gospel of Matthew, the inspired message is spoken in language that brings the mystery closer to human family life: the birth of a child to a husband and his wife. It was the language of an angel who informed Joseph in a dream that Mary, his betrothed, would bear a son who would be called Jesus for "he will save his people from their sins." This announcement to Joseph was followed immediately by reference to the prophetic promise of salvation and grace.

Now all this happened in order to make come true what the Lord had said through the prophet, "A virgin will become pregnant and have a son, and he will be called Immanuel" (which means, "God is with us"). (Matthew 1:22–23)

Remarkably, our wonderings about the incomprehensibilities of God and the ineptness of language are somehow put out of mind when we accept the simple meaning of that statement and realize that no other meaning will do: "God is with us."

A human child is born and at once God is present. The impossible gap between human and divine life is not an impossible gap now, because God is with us. That's what the mystery of the Incarnation means for us as we live our lives day by day.

From a practical point of view, the great mystery of the Incarnation is the presence of God in the ordinary affairs of human life: God is with us. And in the practical ministry of a visitor, the great mystery of blessing in the presence of one human being to another is explained in the same way: God is with us. The Incarnation gives meaning to the word "presence" in the work of ministry. It gives meaning to the challenge of living the gospel for regular folks, finding God in the infinitesimal moments of our every day.

Unfortunately, we can believe in the incarnational presence and still not know it in the ordinary experiences of life. But that is where it will be found. Pastoral ministers can be misled by a zealous desire to "sanctify the moment" or make the blessing present in misfortune, hardship, pain, suffering. Faith tells us that the blessing is already there and only in faith can we know it. According to Elizabeth Dreyer, "our task as Christians is not to 'bring' Christ to the world but to be on the lookout, to discover and uncover the Christ that is already present." How else can we make sense of the words of Jesus?

When I was sick, you visited me . . .
as long as you did it to the least of mine, you did it to me.

We discover the Christ who is already there in a particular way, but in a way that is ordinary. The ability to be present to another's reality when we visit the sick and the dying and attend to them and to those who love them is a way of expecting God to communicate his presence and intentionality in human relationships.

Walking this path in life and serving others in the presence of God may seem to be the kind of life reserved for very special people: spiritual and holy people. We are, as baptized children of God, that special people. We identify ourselves as "the people of God" and know we are called to live the gospels. There is no other way for us to live the gospels than to live in that presence and to "discover and uncover the Christ already present" in our midst, present in us and present in every other child of God. The spirituality of Saint Ignatius speaks to this reality when it challenges us to find God in all things, to live contemplation in the midst of our busy lives, especially in our active ministry.

This chapter will explore the concept of presence and how it happens in pastoral ministry. Presence is not only a concept to be understood; it is a gift that needs to be given. Because it is at the heart of ministry and the core of empathic response, presence is the most important gift a visitor can bring to the sick and to the dying.

Presence of God

The words of Isaiah take the presence of God out of a dry and abstract context and throw it into the middle of personal human life to mix with all of life's anxieties and concerns. No matter what may happen in life, there is the promise of divine presence: I shall be with you.

> Do not be afraid, for I have redeemed you;
> I have called you by name, you are mine.
> Should you pass through the waters, I shall be with you;
> or through the rivers, they will not swallow you up.
> Should you walk through fire, you will not suffer,
> and the flames will not burn you,
> for I am Yahweh, your God,
> the Holy One of Israel, your Savior. (Isaiah 43:1–3)

It is always difficult to remember that God is with us in all things. Even in moments of happiness and joy, we may neglect to share our celebration with the divine presence. But it's even harder, and sometimes impossible, to remember and to believe in that promise that "I shall be with you" in moments of danger.

A person who has just been diagnosed with heart disease, cancer, or AIDS or someone who has just been informed of a tragic loss because of an accident or death often experiences loneliness and abandonment. How can he or she believe in that promise "I shall be with you" when it seems that no one is present at all? When a caregiver tries to be truly present and to offer the gift of compassionate presence to another human being in need, the divine presence breaks through loneliness and abandonment and makes the promise real in the flesh and blood of human life. In his incarnational presence, Christ is the energy behind our desire to help and the grace to accomplish our desire.

Strong in his own faith and certain of the divine presence that accomplished the good works in his own life, St. Paul encouraged all of us who believe to be certain of the divine presence that accomplishes the good works we do.

> It is by grace that you have been saved, through faith; not by anything of your own, but by the gift from God; not by anything that you have done, so that nobody can claim the credit. We are God's work of art, created in Christ Jesus for the good works which God has already designated to make up our way of life. (Ephesians 2:8–10).

We are God's work of art. By baptism we are called to bring the good news of the active presence of God to others. But it is Christ, present by grace and active in the work of human life, who cares for, comforts, consoles, heals, strengthens, and provides for any need of those who turn to him in faith.

When I think of the active presence of God in my own life, I recall an experience I had several years ago. I was fully conscious and lying on a narrow, hard, hospital table and I was able to move only my head during a five-hour electrophysiological study of my heart. With my body fixed in that position, my eyes watched the fascinating inner world of my own heart as it flashed on a TV screen above my head. In a room with doctors busy, watching and consulting, and with nurses listening and responding to the doctors' needs, I was alone in my thoughts and fears.

Initially I tried to be "appropriately curious" and follow the catheters as they crawled through my veins and into the chamber of my heart. Skillfully, doctors tried to construct a "map" of the elaborate electrical wiring system of my heart so they could control the viral-induced malady, ventricular tachycardia, or V. Tach., as it is referred to in medical settings. "So this is what I look like, from the inside out," I thought to myself.

After several hours, the "Star Wars" quality of the surgical theater with its huge circular lights and the cameras moving over my chest induced in me a welter of bone-chilling emotions. Frustration, anger, anxiety, and loss washed over me like a tidal wave. Then, finally, in a way that was not conscious, I moved into a state of numbness to compensate for the trauma of the situation. I felt nothing as I waited for the next invasion of my reality.

During all that time, the caring and the attentiveness of the doctors and the sensitive presence of my cardiologists gave new meaning to my understanding of presence. If these men, who were so intent on their skill and their science, could still be present to me and to my needs, must not God in his mercy be present to me? This was the question that formed in my mind as the time wore on and as my back felt it would break if I didn't soon have the opportunity to move.

Simultaneously, a flood of fear rose within me. I feared that I would never get over the experience or escape this life-threatening situation. After a period of time, the words of the psalmist came to me: "Be still and know that I am God." I reflected on those words, and they gave me peace.

Be still, be still, and be still. Physically, I couldn't move. But my mind and my spirit were not still; they were waging war. Over and over I prayed the words until stillness came and I could begin to hear the message within: "God is present. He is in charge of your life. He will not leave you, for you believe in his words, 'You are precious in my sight and I love you.'"

This was an experience of intense feeling and shocking realization. It was a feeling of literally tasting my mortality and a realization of the fragility of life as my heart was laid out before my eyes, death stood close at my side. But it was also a profoundly spiritual experience for me. It was an experience of learning to place my heart and my life in the hands of others, in the hands of the doctors and ultimately in the hands of God. Dreadful as it was, the experience taught me the meaning of real presence. In the gentle presence of the doctors who cared for me I encountered the unfailing presence of God whose "eye is ever on the sparrow," and ever on me.

Presence to Self

In order to be present to another person, we first must be present to ourselves. It is easy to give a definition of presence as simply "to be there." But a more complete understanding of what it means to be "fully there," in body, mind, and spirit, requires an ability to be, first of all, "at home" with yourself. In other words, you must not only be there for someone else; you must also be there for you.

Being present to oneself in a situation with another person presumes a certain degree of self-knowledge and is, in itself, an aspect of growth in self-knowledge. Self-knowledge, knowing oneself as best as one can, enables a pastoral visitor to attend effectively to another person and be actively conscious of the presence of God. In order to attain this self-knowledge for the sake of ministry, the pastoral visitor must attend to himself or herself as well as to the other person. The same empathy, attending, and respect which must be given to another person must also be given to the self. The ability to be a self-in-relation, which is at the heart of the ministry of visitation, begins with a keen sense of self-presence.

Self-knowledge is necessary to have and difficult to acquire. When it is right there for us to see, we want to look for it in another place. Thomas Keating relates a Sufi tale describing the difficulty we have finding self-knowledge when we search for it.

> A Sufi master lost the key to his house and was outside looking for it on the grass. He got down on his hands and knees and started running his fingers through every blade of grass. Along came eight or ten of his disciples. They said, "Master, what are you doing?" "I have lost the key to my house," he said. "Can we help you find it?" they asked. He said, "I'd be delighted."
>
> So they all started the search—on hands and knees scouring the grass. As the sun grew hotter, one of the more intelligent disciples said, "Master, have you any idea where you might have lost the key?" The master replied, "Of course, I lost it in the house." To which they all exclaimed, "Then why are we looking for it out here?" He said, "Isn't it obvious? There's more light here."

What is "obvious" to us, of course, is the foolishness of searching for something in the wrong place. It may be a diligent search, but it won't succeed. So often we fail to look inside the house ourselves. We search for the answers in the wrong places. We seek light from outside for answers that can be seen only within.

A pastoral visitor dealing with the sadness of death, pain in sickness, and distress in families must "look inside the house," and first of all be present to himself or herself. When we know our own fears, our own pain, our own history, we can become attentive to the fears, pain, and history of someone else. If this has not been done, if we do not look within ourselves, then that deficiency will block the usefulness of pastoral ministry. Such a failure is unavoidable, because we use a lot of energy to attend to our own emotional distress, leaving little or no energy to give to anyone else during a pastoral visit.

For this reason, it is unwise to put off self-knowledge until we face distress or anxiety in pastoral visitation. It's extremely difficult for a pastoral visitor who has not fully attended to his or her own loss of a child, close relative, or friend to be present to a person facing the same grief. It's very hard for a pastoral visitor who has not attended to his or her own thoughts about personal mortality to attend to a person who is facing an imminent death.

Learning to be present to oneself is a life-long process, but, for the sake of pastoral ministry, it is a process that cannot be put off or neglected. We cannot wait until we "have it all together" before we begin our search for self-knowledge, nor can we wait for that to happen before we begin our ministry. The ministry itself will reveal aspects of self-knowledge to us. Sometimes it may happen consciously and outwardly, while at other times it may happen through a deeper search within ourselves. But an attentive preparation for self-knowledge is necessary and will assist us in our active presence to others in the ministry of visitation.

There are, fortunately, spiritual practices that can help us advance in the ability to be present to ourselves, thereby enlarging our ability to be present to another person. They include: self-knowledge, the practice of silence, self-reflection, prayer and contemplation, personal accountability and responsibility. Conducted within the context of personal faith in the Incarnation at work in active silence, these spiritual practices deepen our awareness of the divine presence in pastoral ministry.

Self-knowledge is the goal of the ancient philosophical advice "know thyself." People in the past have understood that self-knowledge ought to increase with age and that it is the appropriate achievement of those advanced in wisdom. For that reason, in addition to personal life experience, reading and study open doors for us into the experience of others and the wisdom of the ages. Progress in the work of self-knowledge takes place also in the processes of counseling, therapy, spiritual direction, and group therapy. Through whatever process, self-knowledge is facilitated and enriched by the company of another who is willing to be with you as you make the journey of life.

The practice of silence is obviously important whenever it is necessary to be present to the world outside the self. It is equally important whenever it is desirable to be present to the world inside the self. Learning to be comfortable with silence is an invitation for another self to speak, to be expressive, and to communicate what is going on in his or her hidden and unique world. Learning to be comfortable in silence is an invitation for your own self to speak, to be expressive, and to communicate what is going on in the hidden and unique world of your own being. Within a context of faith, the practice of silence, which makes us "feel at home both with silence and in silence," is a quiet and active presence that allows us to go beyond the surface to a deeper place where the presence of God waits for us to come.

Self-reflection may be described as the after-thought of silence. This is not to suggest it is less important or does not deserve attention for its own sake. Rather, it is to note its sequential relationship to silence; serious self-reflection can happen only in that place where the "sounds of silence" can first be heard. Self-reflection is the "thought" that comes after silence. With respect to importance, however, self-reflection certainly takes first place. In the practice of self-reflection, we put a hold on the activities of life, the duties and responsibilities, the trivialities and distractions, in order to sort them out and to discover what value and meaning they have for us in the ultimate purpose for our living.

Prayer and contemplation are commonly mentioned together in the guidelines for a spiritual life, because they are parallel pathways, leading in the same direction and with the same destination in view. Prayer is a deliberate turning of our mind and heart toward God and contemplation is a deliberate concentration of our attention on God. Prayer might be more like a magnet, if we imagined a magnet that had only one direction toward God and that no matter what we were doing, thinking, saying, or desiring, all would be directed toward God. St. Paul spoke of this intentional Christian life when he recommended that whether we eat, sleep, or drink, no matter what we do, we should do it to honor and glorify God. Prayer can take the ordinary events of life, such as work and play and even pain and suffering, and give to them spiritual purpose. In the same way, contemplation can take the ordinary things of life, such as flowers and sunsets, and especially people, beautiful or plain or happy or sad, and see within them the imprint of God. Contemplation enables us to experience a moment fully and be mindful of the presence of God in the moment. Saint Paul describes the mystical dimension of contemplation as knowing God "face to face" (1 Corinthians 13:12). Prayer and contemplation are so important that they deserve time reserved for them alone, but at all times we can make them part of the life we live.

Accountability and responsibility are obligations that flow necessarily from our acceptance of the role of pastoral minister. Because they derive from the sacred trust of ministry, they involve much more than fulfillment of the ordinary requirements that are expected in the role of visitor, requirements of courtesy, such as dependability and punctuality. Rather, they come from vocation, from a sacred calling, and in that sense they become privileges that the pastoral minister has been given to perform for his or her own benefit as well as for the benefit of the person in sickness or distress. Ministers need contact on a regular basis with a supervisor, a confidant or friend, or a group of colleagues with whom they can share their personal concerns, work through mutual problems, and engage in common prayer. Prudent and confidential help from capable advisors provides protection for both the visitor and the patient. The visit will more likely be effective and the visitor will less likely suffer burnout.

Presence to Others

The theological foundations for the presence of God in the suffering and the bereaved can be found in the writings of Karl Rahner. Rahner believes there are intrinsic connections between human experience and the ultimate mystery we call God. If we share that same belief, we can understand that there is mystery lying beneath the events of human life and will be prepared "to see" the mystery with the eyes of faith. Living a spirituality of everyday life, the pastoral visitor has a sacred mission "to see" the presence of God, to uncover the mystery lying beneath the ordinary events that take place in ministry.

Such an experience happened in my life many years ago, but it was not until after the event took place that my own belief brought me into contact with the mystery of divine presence hidden there. On the first day of my new job as director of a pastoral care department in a hospital, I was asked by the nurse in charge of neonatal care to visit a thirty-five-year-old woman who had given birth to an infant boy born with spina bifida. The mother refused to see her baby.

Even though she refused to see her baby, I observed the depth of her feelings of loss and of pain, and I observed that her anger at God was profound. For years, the couple had tried to conceive a child, and now that they had succeeded and brought the child to birth, they knew that they would soon lose their beautiful son. God had given to them, and now God would take away from them. The joy of the gift elated them and the pain of the loss shattered them.

My role as a pastoral minister was to be present to the couple and share in the feelings that were overwhelming them, to share in the tears that expressed their grief, a grief that grew stronger as the death of the child grew nearer. After a few days, the mystery lying beneath this sad birth began to break through for the couple. It was a mystery still not understood but accepted in the conviction of faith. The mother agreed to take her child in her arms, to look at him, to hold him in her love and prepare to let him go in death. Watching the mother hold her precious baby, watching her gaze on him in love and seeing her suffer as the priest baptized her innocent child was a sacred moment in time for me. A few hours later, the baby died.

In the solitude of my office, I burst into tears. From the depths of my soul, I cried. For me, too, there was mystery in this event that touched my life, a mystery hidden in the surge of feelings that rose from deep within me. Only when I was able to sort out the feelings did I remember something that happened years previously and was waiting to be uncovered by me in that sacred moment. My younger sister, too, had been born with spina bifida. She had lived for just one month. For the first time, I realized what it must have been like for my parents to lose a child, and for the first time, I got in touch with my own feelings and realized what it was like to lose my sister. The mystery of divine presence lies beneath the events we share in pastoral ministry. Each of us will uncover with his or her own eyes of faith the meaning each one of us alone can see.

The inability to see what another person alone can see or to know what experience awaits us demands a spirit of humility in the practice of pastoral care. A pastoral visitor must approach each place of visitation as a sacred space that holds a mystery of divine grace. When we enter a room where a patient has been alone in silence, we are entering a very private space, a world unknown to us, full of private thoughts and feelings, hopes and fears. We must wait to be invited to enter that world. We can only imagine what has been going on there and what is present in the mind and heart of the person before whom we stand. This is "holy" ground.

Unless we have experienced it for ourselves, we cannot begin to understand the distress of a person who was physically active and is now suddenly unable to move about freely, to choose what to do and where to go. Many people have never known the confinement and constraints of inactivity. Many people have never experienced the solitude and silence it brings. For many people, their first experience of solitude and silence is forced upon them by illness. Pastoral visitors must strive to be always conscious of the reality of what they do not know. They must be mindful of the stress, the anxiety, and the depth of fear often unspoken that is present in the hearts of the patients they visit. By attentive presence to that reality of the unknown, a sensitive visitor can help a patient to articulate those concerns, put words to the feelings, share the burden, and so let the healing of mind and soul begin.

It is impossible to overestimate the importance of the unknown dimension that stands between the pastoral visitor and the patient, and that can make the difference between unbearable distress and tender healing. My own experience in ministry with a teenager, a young sixteen-year-old boy, gave to me the gift and the privilege of discovering the power of the mystery that stood for a while between him and me. Attentive pastoral care which is simply true empathic presence to another person enabled him to become aware of what was present deep in his own spirit, enabling it to become a power for healing his distress.

His parents had brought their teenage football player to the emergency room because he was suffering from symptoms that seemed like the flu. After hours of testing, the parents heard news more dreadful than they had expected. It was not the flu which afflicted their son, but leukemia. His illness was not an inconvenient sickness but a fatal disease that would shorten his life. The news that was painfully distressing for his parents was frightening and totally disabling for the boy. In an attempt to escape from it, he fled. Having heard the words of the doctor, the frightened boy ran out of the hospital and down the street.

He came back again. However, for days and months he continued to run—not down the street, but into his own private space with his own thoughts and fears. He ran to be alone. He refused to hear the words that were chasing him. He refused to leave that world where he was alone with his school and his football and his family and his friends, a world where nothing would change. During one full year of my daily visits, this lonely teenager would not invite me or anyone else into his private world. He refused to accept his diagnosis and insisted that soon he would be playing football again.

For me, it was a year of daily visits with nothing to bring to him but presence and nothing to do for him but wait. Finally, he spoke words that invited me to share his thoughts and his fears, where he was no longer alone with them. "I know I am dying," he said. "I know it and I am scared to death." In that moment, the barrier was lifted and we were truly present to each other. We could be together in the moment honestly and accept it exactly as it was. So we laughed. We laughed at his choice of words. We laughed because he said he was "scared to death," and we both knew it was a funny thing to try to blame fright for his death.

With the unknown no longer standing between us, once he had acknowledged the reality of his fear of death and his awareness that it was close upon him, we were able to speak openly about his illness and what he must expect from it. During one of those conversations, I asked him, "What would you really want to do? What would you really want to do, if only you had the opportunity to do it?" He thought about this for a while. Then he said to me, "I would love to be able to go to Disney World with my sister."

Illness of any kind is systemic and is not confined to the individual who suffers from it. It afflicts in some way every other human being who is attached to the sick person. Terminal illness in a young person who has hopes and desires for a future that will never be is a systemic problem that has the power to bring together an entire community of people. In the case of this young man, everyone in the hospital felt close to him.

They knew him and grew to love him. His "dream wish" became their dream wish, so the nurses, staff, and doctors collected money for his trip to Disney World. Their response was really an extension of their attentive presence to him. Just as they were "with" him in the expectation of his death, they wanted to be "with" him in the fulfillment of his dream. When his next period of remission set in, he did the one thing he wanted to do "if only he had the opportunity to do it." Full of joy, he left the hospital with his sister for Disney World. He returned to the hospital, and his condition got worse. Within two months, he died.

While he lived through his illness to its end, this young man at first separated himself from the love and care he deserved and needed. Without knowing any better, he retreated from any attentive presence of his family and his medical caregivers and from my pastoral care as well. He searched for comfort in loneliness where no comfort could be found, because no attentive presence was there for him. In the ministry of pastoral visitation, the visitor must respect the separation but never interrupt the ministry, never fail to be there with attentive presence. In my estimation, it was the loving presence of the hospital community and their willingness to work with the family to embrace this young man with an experience of "lived presence" that helped him to emerge from his loneliness and face his fear and his death. Whatever comfort and blessing our loving silent presence gave to him, it gave as much to all those who were part of it with him.

Understanding presence intellectually is relatively easy, but being open to the experience of "incarnational presence" actually at work in ministry is a challenge of faith. It is a challenge of faith daily to believe that the face of God is present in ordinary faces and in the ordinary places. It is a challenge of faith to believe that, even in silence, the voice of God speaks and the incarnational presence of God's love heals.

To find the presence of God in ministry and see the image of God in another person—the poor, the sick, the imprisoned, the oppressed, and the suffering people of the world—is a gift given to us in baptism. It is our vocation as people of God to be a community and to live our lives joined together as a family of faith. Illness and suffering in a family are systemic, and as members of the Christian family, we are never sick alone and we never suffer alone. Here is what Elizabeth Dreyer says about our identity as a "priestly people":

> We do not stand alone. In community, the priestly "I" becomes
> the priestly "we." Through this priesthood, we actively partici-
> pate in history by noticing the worldly face of God in its agony
> and in its joy, and by lifting up together all of creation.

If we accept that interpretation of Christian community, then we must accept the priestly obligation to "actively participate" in Christian community. No matter where we find ourselves, "we do not stand alone" because we belong in Christian community.

Knowing that one belongs in community imposes on a pastoral minister the obligation to understand what it means to be truly present to another person and what it means to be truly present to oneself. Janet Ruffing explains this dynamic and emphasizes its importance as spiritual preparation for ministry.

> Presence means being at home in ourselves, fully there If we are preoccupied with our worries, our grief, our "to do" lists, we are separated, cut off from the present moment and the deeper reality of God's presence and of anyone or anything else. To be present means to be consciously experiencing, noticing and responding. It is an experience of mutuality in that we are open to another as well as ourselves, consciously available to being affected by another.

Ruffing makes it very clear that the spiritual dimension of Christian community requires an awareness of "the deeper reality of God's presence," and that this awareness is not possible until we learn that we live in relationship. Each one of us is a self-in-relation. Human life is not lived in separation, and separation is not "human" life. There is profound spiritual truth in the poetic assertion of John Donne that "no man is an island" and that as human beings we cannot really live in isolation from one another. Christian community is a mutuality of openness to the relationship we have with one another as human beings, and Christian community is a mutuality of openness to "the deeper reality of God's presence" which is, for people of faith, the mystery of the Incarnation at work in active silence.

References

Dreyer, Elizabeth A. (1994). *Earth Crammed with Heaven*. Mahwah, N.J.: Paulist Press.

Keating, Thomas (1999). *The Human Condition*. Mahwah, N.J.: Paulist Press.

The New Jerusalem Bible (1985). New York: Doubleday.

Rahner, Karl (1978). *Foundations of Christian Faith: An Introduction to the Idea of Christianity.* New York: Seabury Press.

Ruffing, Janet (2000). "Socially Engaged Contemplation: Living Contemplatively in Chaotic Times." In Wicks, Robert J., ed., *Handbook of Spirituality for Ministers,* Vol. 2, pp. 418–441. Mahwah, N.J.: Paulist Press.

For Further Reading

Dreyer, Elizabeth A., ed. (2000). *The Cross in Christian Tradition.* Mahwah, N.J.: Paulist Press.

Downey, Michael (1997). *Understanding Christian Spirituality.* Mahwah, N.J.: Paulist Press.

Harper, Ralph (1991). *On Presence.* Philadelphia: Trinity Press International.

Nouwen, Henri J. M. (1990). *Beyond the Mirror.* New York: Crossroad Publishing Company.

Soelle, Dorothee (1995). *Theology for Skeptics.* Minneapolis: Fortress Press.

Sulmasy, Daniel P. (1997). *The Healer's Calling.* Mahwah, N.J.: Paulist Press.

Shelp, Earl E., & Sunderland, R. H. (2000). *Sustaining Presence.* Nashville: Abingdon Press.

Walters, Kerry (2001). *Practicing Presence.* Franklin, Wis.: Sheed & Ward.

The Costly Business
of Being a Care Partner

Beverly Anne Musgrave

Lois Brown, a tall, thin woman with compassionate, sad eyes, is a schoolteacher. And, like all schoolteachers with full-time jobs, she begins her day early in the morning. Actually, however, she begins her day of teaching late the night before. Not until then can she find time in the few hours remaining before midnight to catch up on all the other work that teachers do for the next day: preparing for class, correcting papers, reading reports, and calculating grades. With not enough rest during the night, she will rise early again in the morning for another long hard day of teaching math to eleventh-grade students. Her daily routine is not the result of procrastination, disorganization, lethargy, or any kind of deficiency on her part. It's the result of her decision to dedicate her entire day to doing "the best she can," all the while knowing that "the best she can" is not, could not, and never will be good enough.

In addition to having a full-time job as a schoolteacher, Lois Brown is wife, lover, friend, and companion to her husband of thirty years. That relationship is not only the most precious part of her life, but it has become another full-time job. Just as she does "the best she can" in her profession as schoolteacher, Lois struggles to do "the best she can" in her full-time job with her husband. However, there's simply not enough time in one day for all of the things required to do a good job in both of them.

The burden carried by this loving wife and conscientious teacher is not unusual. It's a common burden for her and anyone else who must fulfill the role of care partner for a family member or loved one. A person trying to be two things at once is stretched to give time and energy far beyond what any one person can give.

At the age of fifty-seven, Lois's husband is a frail man who no longer has the robust physical body that served him well as chief of the Fire Department. He is dying of cancer. With the prospect of only a few remaining years of companionship ahead of them, Lois and her husband cherish the time they can spend together. Yet, even though she plans carefully, trying to steal time for both of them and for her work, she never has any time for herself. She gently and patiently attends to her husband's needs, late into the night, listens attentively to words that will connect them, and finally prepares him for bed and shares his hope for a restful night. During this quiet time she struggles with her anger, her disappointment, her guilt, and her fears of a future without him. Early in the morning, she awakens to organize the detailed agenda she must negotiate with a professional caregiver who arrives at 7 A.M. to "take over" when Lois leaves for school.

Except for the specific details of her work and home life, Lois Brown is a good example of the way millions of people live their lives today. In a recent issue, the periodical *Wellness Matters* reported that "today it is estimated that there are between eighteen and twenty-five million Americans caring for a chronically ill family member at home." That statement, "caring for a chronically ill family member at home," is deceptively simple, until one considers all the implications attached to each one of the important words included in it: "caring for," "chronically ill," "family member," "at home."

I want to point out some of those implications that deserve more careful consideration and to indicate some of the consequences that are likely to become part of the daily lives of those eighteen to twenty-five million people. "Caring for" the sick is ordinarily a task for a person trained to perform it. Caring for the "chronically ill" is, indeed, a specialized aspect of professional training. It's a devastating experience when a "family member" becomes chronically ill, but it's even more distressing when another family member must himself or herself assume responsibility for the care of that family member. Finally, chronic illness "at home" requires daily attention without hospital personnel at hand to provide advice and assistance; at unpredictable moments it may also require treatment procedures that are better performed in a hospital setting. Taken together, all these considerations are enormously burdensome for the family of a chronically ill person who needs care at home.

There is another statistic that can't be ignored when we look at the way American society provides care for the sick and dying. Recently, Patricia Braus cited a report showing that the burden is not distributed evenly among family members. According to the report, women make up 73 percent of all caregivers. A gross imbalance in our cultural perspective automatically gives women the responsibility for care giving at home. Because of an impulse of nature, or the pressure of social norms, or perhaps simply by default, women frequently find themselves left with the duty. In our traditional social structure, women are brought up to be the family's primary caregiver and, willy-nilly, they must accept that role and all the hardships that go with it.

Who Is a Care Partner?

While the role of care partner can be described with some precision, it's virtually impossible to describe the extraordinary variety of people who do it. There are eighteen to twenty-five million faces to describe, and there are eighteen to twenty-five million stories to tell. Aside from the fact that the overwhelming majority of them are women, an adequate description must include many differences in age, education, financial situation, personal health, family assistance, professional ability, available time, and many other circumstances that will affect their performance.

Of course, some are trained professionals who provide care as a means of daily employment. They are professionals with specified duties, and they have been taught ways of dealing with emotional and physical stress. But this is not the case when the caregiver is simply a family member. Even when professional care is available to a family, it never completely satisfies the need for care. Someone else—wife or husband, daughter or son, other family member, friend or neighbor—must step into the role and fill the gap when a professional can't be there or goes home at the end of the day. This chapter will focus on the "someone else" who takes on the role and carries out the duties as family caregiver or as caring visitor for the sick person.

It has already been emphasized that the primary concern of the ministry of visitation is the patient, and that the attentive presence of the minister is rightly directed toward the patient. However, we've also seen that illness is systemic, and it follows that the attention of the minister needs to be directed toward others who are part of that system. In the course of a routine visit to a hospital patient or to a nursing home resident or to a homebound patient, the caring visitor will most likely meet that "someone else" who is the family caregiver. It is appropriate for the visitor to recognize the systemic aspects of caring for the patient and take into account the diversity of beliefs and values represented in the family system.

Waiting, Watching, Hoping

If Lois Brown is representative of all caregivers, then it's clear that time is a major concern for them. All of their willingness and determination and strength of spirit are challenged by the inexorable clicking of the clock. It is not only the scarcity of time that makes them anxious, but also the need to make difficult choices and to apportion the time right among the changing and necessary tasks of each day. It's simply "the way things are."

The "time to be born" and "the time to die" come at their own invitation, but what about all the time in between? This question can become a torment for a caregiver who is aware that time is gradually stealing away the strength and life of a beloved family member. The "weight of time" is a reality that each and every caregiver comes face to face with each day.

One day in the life of a caregiver is like every other day. They are all filled with the same thing. Waiting, watching, and hoping consume one day and spill over into the next. With merely incidental changes, the story of every caregiver resembles each day in the life of Lois Brown, the full-time teacher and full-time caregiver. At the end of the day, weary and bone-tired, she sits by her husband and waits. She attends to his needs and very carefully she watches him to see what else she might do to give him comfort. No matter what her mind knows about his illness, in her heart she keeps on hoping.

For Lois Brown, the activities of the day may change, but as the family caregiver her obligation is always the same: to wait, to watch, and to hope. The waiting is a mixed experience. Love relationships often carry veiled anger and resentment that has not been worked through. Unable to speak of this deeper pain, she speaks aloud to him of the private pleasures and joy-filled experiences they've shared. But does he remember what is so vivid in her mind? A faint smile of recollection seems to cross his worn face and leaves her with a doubt. She wonders, "Does he hear me?" With measured care, she tells him that both of their adult children will be visiting for the weekend and hopes he will be happy to see them again. Does he understand? Questions always come to her, and they seem always to be the same: Does he hear? Does he understand? Can I, should I express my negative feelings? Does he know how much I love him?

Lois hopes and trusts that what she wants to believe is true—that he does hear and understand and that her presence by the bed is a joy for him and that her caring is a comfort to him. She hears the chimes of the clock strike twelve: the end of another busy day of care giving and the beginning of another silent night of vigil. Wrapped in a blanket, she falls asleep in her favorite chair at his bedside.

Whether during the day or during the night, the waiting and the watching and the hoping can become wearisome and feel interminable, especially when the signs of hope and trust grow dim. It's then that the stillness of God penetrates the spirit and can release feelings that the heart has kept locked inside because they are too dreadful to acknowledge. In the stillness they may demand to be accepted for what they are. They may be named *resignation* or *acceptance* or *peacefulness* and be expressed in quiet prayer, "Thy will be done." They may be named *anger, defiance,* or *despair* and be expressed in raging doubt, "My God, my God, why have you forsaken me?" Whatever resolution may come from the stillness, the spiritual ministry of the care partner can be a sign of hope and trust for the brokenhearted caregiver and help to renew a faltering faith in the loving and healing presence of God.

The Systemic Aspects of Illness

The debilitating effects of illness on a patient during the struggle with disease are surely apparent, and the outcome of a long-term illness resulting in death is obvious to everyone. What is not always apparent and is often ignored, however, is the profound impact illness and death have on the significant people in the life of the sick or dying person. Murray Bowen says that "no life event can stir more emotionally directed thinking in the individual and more emotional reactiveness in those about him" than being present to the one who is loved and witnessing that person's suffering.

Illness has a ripple effect that moves beyond the family and is far-reaching in its impact. It ripples into the broader communities to which the sick person belongs. It touches church members, co-workers, neighbors, friends, and to some extent the world at large. The consequences of illness are more far-reaching and long-lasting than even those closely related to the sick person themselves realize.

This being true, it is not unusual that a tangle of mental perceptions and emotional responses may develop within the various interrelated systems for which the sick person is the focus of attention. If the visiting care partner can encourage each person to own his or her own feeling, this will greatly assist the family members to deal with personal issues of guilt and anger and possibly help to disentangle the troubling mix of emotional responses among the family members. The experience of illness may then become a context for relational change between the patient and family members and/or between family members themselves.

It must be cautioned, however, that the visitor is not a therapist, and it is important for him or her to maintain clear boundaries. In some instances, differentiation will be essential for healing family dysfunction when, for example, the family members are experiencing an emotional stuck-togetherness rooted in quiet, unspoken, and unresolved feelings of guilt—the husband or wife experiencing guilt for a secret affair, the children experiencing guilt for not visiting, supporting, or caring for the parent. All together, the family members have created a trap enmeshing them in the bonds of self-blame and recrimination cast from one to another.

In difficult family situations, a visiting care partner can offer to all family members a "holding environment," a safe and non-judgmental space where attentive listening is encouraged and free expression of thoughts and feelings is allowed. The ability of the visiting care partner to listen attentively, to hold the tension, and to understand the different points of view expressed will encourage everyone else involved to be attentive and understanding. Most important, perhaps, if the visitor manages to be empathically engaged without becoming emotionally enmeshed—in other words, to be a differentiated person—he or she will help the patient and other family members to respond to their specific and personal roles as caregivers.

The Role of Forgiveness

Modeled by a visiting care partner and imitated by the family caregiver and other family members, empathic listening can bring about relational changes within the family system. These relational changes can improve the emotional climate in which the patient must live out his or her sickness. Possibly the most important area here is forgiveness: the willingness to seek forgiveness when it is needed and the willingness to grant forgiveness when it is asked.

Forgiveness is a cure for the suffering of guilt. From a spiritual point of view, it is absolutely essential to restore love and belonging into broken relationships. Where forgiveness is lacking, the disquiet and disease of the spirit can become more debilitating and disabling than the illness itself. Over a long period of time, the obstinate refusal to ask for it or to give forgiveness squanders the power of forgiveness to heal and strengthens the power of un-forgiveness to hurt. Nothing but forgiveness has the power to heal hurts and to overcome grievances.

My own experience as a director of the pastoral care department in a hospital some time ago revealed that wisdom working in real life. It was my first meeting with a dying patient and her family in my pastoral ministry there, but it is an experience that has stayed with me through the years. One night I waited with Nancy, an angry, tired, visibly distressed woman, who was anxiously trying to summon up her courage to go into the room where her sister Ginny was dying. She needed courage to enter the room—not the courage we all need to meet death face to face, but courage to meet her sister face to face. They both needed the courage we all need so often in life to ask for and to give forgiveness.

For twenty years the sisters had not met, had not spoken to each other to say the difficult and painful words that would ask for and allow forgiveness back into their lives. Instead, they had lived in fear and with the difficult and painful realization that they were separated. Now death was about to bring a separation they had no power to breach. Sadly, Nancy told me that she did not know how to begin, because she did not know what wrong needed to be put right. "You know," she said, "I have no idea what the falling out was about. I don't even know why we have been so angry with each other. It seems so insignificant now."

But she wanted to begin. She wanted to visit her sister, if I would accompany her. Even though we did not know what to expect, we entered the room. Ginny looked very frail. Her eyes were closed and her breathing was ragged. She slowly opened her eyes and, when she saw her sister, a weak, pained smile covered her wrinkled face and tears splashed on her pillow. Finally, they were together as sisters, and they spoke to each other and asked forgiveness. They were together for one brief hour after twenty years of separation. In a precious moment beyond the hour, at one minute after six o'clock, Ginny died. Death would separate Ginny and Nancy, but, at the moment of Ginny's death, the sisters' hands were clasped in forgiveness.

Twenty years of painful, angry separation is a high price to pay for any injury great or small, but especially for a grievance that cannot even be remembered and "seems so insignificant now." But, if truth be told, twenty years did not make it "seem" insignificant but revealed what it had always been—insignificant. Human perversity and stubbornness can cheat us into spreading over twenty years the healing that can happen in an hour or even a minute of forgiveness.

Regrettably, not all negative relationships are healed before death, and not all family members and friends have the opportunity for reconciliation before death. In many families, bitterness and fighting intensify and add grievances and hurts that are greatly out of proportion to the original injury. What was an already painful situation at the beginning can become a deeply distressing separation at the end. It is worthwhile repeating what has already been said about the importance of the visiting care partner to model behavior in the family setting. At these moments, a chaplain or caring visitor has a privileged objective position and can help the family members to create a "holding environment" which will provide time so that reconciliation can take place.

Everyone involved in the family system must work to maintain stability in their relationships and not let them break apart under the strain of disagreement or misunderstanding. Human emotional suffering, in all of its guises, is the experience that human beings have when they know that deep down inside themselves they are not capable or simply not willing to reach out to one another in loving forgiveness. Because this is true, our human emotional suffering will be healed only when we find a place deep down inside ourselves for forgiveness to grow so that it can begin to repair the broken relationships that have kept us apart.

Caregivers or care partners often remember the things they were unable to do for the sick person and the moments when they felt that they could not cope with the illness. Such memories reveal our human inadequacy. It is a given—the finite self stands face to face with human limitations. At such low times, the care partner himself or herself needs caring attention from the pastoral visitor who is the only one there who can be genuinely empathetic, who can "walk in the shoes" of the care partner and understand the inadequacy.

In order to be attentive in that way, the caring visitor must make an effort to feel, know, and to accept the unique but interrelated experiences of the care partner and of the patient. The "holy ground" into which the visitor enters in order to find and to see the face of God in the sick person is the same "holy ground" into which the visitor enters to find and to see the face of God in the care partner.

Stress and the Care Partner

Anyone who ignores the stress that ordinary activities can bring into our lives is not a sensible person. Stress is not avoidable in human life, and it is always wise to be aware of its consequences. Ordinarily, the consequences of stress are endured and can be relieved without doing harm when the stress has passed. A list provided by Wayne Weiten identifies what he considers to be the four principal types of stress: frustration, change, conflict, and pressure. The way these types of stress appear, exhibit themselves, and eventually disappear in the life of an individual depends, of course, on the particular kind of activities in which the individual is engaged and on the capacity of the person to deal with that particular kind of stress.

In his definition of stress, Weiten takes into account individual differences, capabilities, and perceptions peculiar to each person. He defines stress as "any circumstances that threaten or are perceived to threaten one's well-being and that thereby tax one's coping abilities." Activities and circumstances that are the ordinary experiences for an Olympic athlete in competition or for a circus wild-animal trainer or for a surgeon on duty in an emergency room don't cause undue stress for them, because they don't threaten or are not perceived to threaten their well-being. The same activities surely would threaten the rest of us; we definitely ought to perceive that they would threaten our well-being. Weiten has made clear in his definition that the *perception* of the individual person is a crucial factor in causing stress, and that individual coping abilities determine the consequences of the stress.

Caregivers can come into daily contact with chronic illness, major illness, and death. Because of the activities they perform and the circumstances in which they provide care to the sick and dying, caregivers will at various times and to a certain extent experience the four principal types of stress and their consequences. Let's take them one-by-one:

There are *frustrations* in the life of a caregiver. The major frustrations often revolve around change. Illness, either chronic or major, introduces *change* not only in the life of the sick person but also in the life of the care partner, often in the form of disruptions with serious consequences. While attending to the needs of a patient, a care partner inevitably encounters *conflict* within himself or herself simply because of ambiguous feelings about taking on the responsibility of caring for a family member, including the thought of the possible loss of a significant other or loved one. Even the changes that a person voluntarily introduces into the patterns of life—changes in marital status, career or work, financial resources—may cause slight stress. The changes that illness and death unexpectedly introduce into life inevitably cause severe stress. It is even more certain that *pressure* will be a day-after-day experience for a care partner: the pressure to know what care to give, the pressure to understand the illness, the pressure simply to be present and to offer hope when hope seems nebulous and slim.

Because of the frustration, the changes, the conflict, and the pressure that cause stress for them, caregivers need to be attentive to their own needs and to care for themselves as well as for the sick person. They must not forget that they are engaged in "the costly business of being a care partner," and they will not get out of it without paying the cost. Sooner or later, they'll discover what the cost is. Often the cost of caring doesn't leave its enduring imprint immediately. When the crisis is over and the stress has lessened, the cost may appear suddenly by surprise and demand payment. For instance, the care partner may find that an over-zealous and imprudent generosity has resulted in irreparable damage to his or her own health and well-being. For anyone in the "costly business" of being a care partner, whether as a family caregiver or as a professional caregiver or as a caring visitor, scrupulous attention to self-needs is critical for personal well-being.

It is not only legitimate to take care of yourself as a care partner, it is an obligation and a spiritual virtue. Taking care of yourself is an act of gratitude to God for your own health and well-being. It is a spiritual virtue to make use of all those things that contribute to health and well-being.

Experts in the fields of physical and psychological health have made many different suggestions for the elimination of stress and the improvement of well-being. Many of these suggestions are overlapping, in the sense that they contribute to the health of both body and spirit. Most obvious, perhaps, but also too often neglected, especially in the role of caregiver, are the obligations to care for the daily needs of the body: the needs for sleep, nutrition, exercise, relaxation, and prompt response to symptoms of physical ailments.

Less obvious, possibly, and more often misunderstood also in the role of caregiver, are the obligations to care for the daily needs of the spirit: the needs for release of pent-up emotions, relaxation procedures, the practice of spiritual disciplines such as meditation and yoga, emotional support and advice in supervision, therapy, and simple recreation. The meeting of these needs can be approached in a more or less intense way, depending on the kinds of stress experienced. Acknowledging that dealing with stress is a primary concern for the caregiver, each person can attend to it in the way that is best for that person. But it is a good and necessary thing to attend to stress. Unacknowledged and unattended stress is always damaging and problematic.

The Cost to Caring

All those who take upon themselves the burden of caring for the sick and the dying have private reasons for doing so. It may be that they do not really know or understand the reasons, except to say they are "good" reasons. If the reasons are truly worthy and just, probably it is not important to name them. But it is important for every caregiver to know and understand that there is a "cost to caring."

Having the opportunity to listen to the "wounded storyteller" and to walk the sacred path of illness and death is a great privilege, but it is a costly one. The scope of this chapter doesn't allow for discussion of all the traumatic complications that may accompany some long-term care giving. However, it is important to note that "compassion fatigue" puts many care partners at risk. In his book titled with the name of the syndrome, Charles Fighey offers guidelines for developing a plan to deal with compassion fatigue.

Under the heading of "personal care," Fighey includes all those aspects of personal life that require a delicate balance in order to avoid either neglect or over-investment in specific dimensions—namely, the physical, the social, and the psychological dimensions. Under the heading of "professional care," Fighey includes everything in career and occupation that is likely to impinge on the balance required to maintain an appropriate separation of professional life from private life—namely, the balance between work and play, the necessity of replenishing body and spirit after the exertions of work, and the absolute necessity of recognizing the impact of loss and grief in life.

Unfortunately, in our society, those dividing lines are not usually recognized and respected, and the consequences of neglect are allowed to intensify. For example, when the death of a family member or significant other occurs, the grieving person is expected to take a few days off to attend a funeral service and to return to work on day three as if nothing of great impact had happened. But something of enormous impact did happen and the traumatic effects of grief continue to make themselves felt well beyond the time allotted to them. This routine manner of dealing with loss doesn't lessen the nature of the impact. The personal, professional, and societal consequences of this way of dealing with death have yet to be recognized and researched.

Hopefully, society will one day recognize and respect the need that we have as human beings to deal with personal loss in different ways. At present it is impossible to estimate how many people share in secret a burden of unrelieved grief, just as did a young man I encountered whose pain and grief were hidden even from himself. It was a brief meeting with a man on a bus, a stranger of about thirty-five years of age. He said that he had recently buried his mother and that, as the only male in the family, he was designated to make all the arrangements for the funeral. Also, he became the executor of the estate.

Preparations for the funeral and attention to family and out-of-town relatives filled up all of the three days the young man was given to be away from work and to grieve for the loss of his mother. He wondered how the brief time had slipped away from him so quickly and yet had changed his life so drastically. But he had to stop his wondering because on the fourth day he was back at his job and was no longer a son grieving for the loss of his mother. He was the CEO of his company and was expected to deal with all the major business problems it was facing. "That was six months ago," he said, "and to this day, I have not had a moment to grieve, not a moment to reflect on what all that has happened to me and to feel my loss, even though my body reflects on my loss every time I move." It would be comforting to suppose that the experience of this young man is not common. But death is common, and this is the all-too-common way in which our society deals with grief, loss, and death.

Loss and Bereavement

When a family care partner experiences grief resulting from the death of a loved one, it is an intense experience that extends over a period of time. Even though it's something universal that happens eventually to everyone, it is always uniquely experienced by each individual. Roslyn Karaban says that "whenever we experience a significant loss, our internal reaction is one of grief. Grief is an unavoidable, spontaneous response to loss. Grief is universal—felt by everyone—and is experienced at many and varied times in our lives. It is an ordinary, everyday occurrence that we all must live through."

If we refer back to the story of Lois Brown, we can see that her grief began with the onset of her husband's illness, when she realized that her life with him was changed forever. The daily losses, the grieving of the shared intimacy no longer possible, the sadness of dreams lost—all of these can be the cause of grieving long before death takes place. While trying to live with the painful reality of terminal illness, Lois Brown and her children already grieve the loss of their relationship with their father and her husband. Their caring visitor, who has become a companion to the patient and shares in his hope, feels the same loss as the family but feels it in a different way. Because the visitor and Lois are care partners in relationship with a sick and dying man, they both feel the loss, they both grieve.

The daily and weekly process of accepting the reality of the loss and the inevitability of experiencing the pain of grief, as well as the adjustment to life without a loved one who is dying, are ongoing challenges which a care partner must be ready to accept each day. Death creates a painful loss and grief will make the loss seem final, leaving an unfillable void. But it is necessary to reinvest in other relationships as well as to cherish the ones that remain. The discovery of meaning in new relationships will be crucial for the ongoing process of integrating grieving into one's life.

Major changes in life point to the "interconnectedness" of everything. A caring visitor needs to develop the ability to discover meaning-making in the midst of grief and to make some sense out of the loss. In order to continue in ministry to the sick and to the dying, a care partner cannot live without his own way of finding hope, even in loss and death and grief. It is something that no one of us can do alone. We need to find for ourselves the other people who are gifts to us, so that we can be gift to one another as we each deal with the unique and universal experiences of loss and bereavement.

Margaret Kornfeld tells us of the sacred experience of listening when she says, "Endings and beginnings that accompany them offer second chances for the uncompleted endings of a former time." This wisdom reminds us that coming to terms with the finite nature of life and listening to the sacred stories of others is truly the greatest and often most difficult gift.

References

"Advice for Caregivers" (1998). *Wellness Matters,* Fall, no. 4.

Bowen, M. (1978). *Family Therapy in Clinical Practice.* New York: Jason Aronsen.

Braus, Patricia (1998). "When the Helper Needs a Hand." *American Demographics, 20* (9), 66–68.

Fighey, Charles (1995). *Compassion Fatigue.* New York: Brunner Mazel.

Karaban, Roslyn (2000). *Complicated Losses, Difficult Deaths.* San Jose, Calif.: Resource Pub. Inc.

Kornfeld, Margaret (2000). *Cultivating Wholeness.* New York: Continuum Press.

Riordan, Margaret (2000). "Avoiding the Hazards to Personal Well Being Inherent in Living with and Caring for our Infirm Parent as an Adult Child." Unpublished M.A. Paper. Fordham University.

Weiten, Wayne (1997). *Psychology: Themes and Variations.* 3rd. ed. Monterey, Calif.: Brooks/Cole.

For Further Reading

Carlsen, Mary Baird (1988). *Meaning Making.* New York: W. W. Norton & Co.

Doka, Kenneth J. (1993). *Living with Life-Threatening Illness: A Guide for Patients, Their Families & Caregivers.* San Francisco: Jossey-Bass Publisher.

Dexter, Pat Egan (1999). *Coping as Caregivers.* Mystic, Conn.: Twenty-Third Publications.

Friedman, Edwin H. (1985). *Generation to Generation.* New York: Guilford Press.

Gorsuch, Nancy J. (1999). *Pastoral Visitation.* Minneapolis: Fortress Press.

Kalish, Richard A. (1985). *Death, Grief and Caring Relationships.* 2nd ed. Monterey, California: Brooks/Cole.

O'Mally, William J., S.J. (1998). *Meeting the Living God.* 3rd ed. Mahwah, N.J.: Paulist Press.

Oliver, Samuel Lee (1998). *What the Dying Teach Us.* New York: Haworth Pastoral Press.

Oates, Wayne E. (1998). *Grief, Transition & Loss: A Pastor's Practical Guide.* Minneapolis: Fortress Press.

Sankar, Andrew (1999). *Dying at Home: A Family Guide for Caregiving.* Baltimore: The John Hopkins University Press.

A Healing Presence:
Meetings with Patients

Jacqueline C. Perez, D.O.

> *The practice of medicine is an art, not a trade; a calling, not a business; a calling in which your heart will be exercised equally with your head.*
> —*Sir William Osler*

Healing is a process by which one is made healthy, whole, or sound of body and mind. Medicine is the art and science of restoring or preserving health through the healing process. The technological achievements of the last century and the development of medical subspecialties and managed care systems have shifted the focus of healing primarily to that of the body, with little or no emphasis placed on the health of the mind and spirit. The spiritual dimension of healing is ignored. More often the body, mind, and spirit are treated as separate entities, with multiple practitioners taking care of their respective areas. This approach conflicts with the healing process of the whole person and creates a gap in the medical care of the patient. In this chapter, three stories recounting visits with patients will be used to begin to look at the spiritual aspects of healing and better define its incorporation in our encounters with people suffering from grief or illness.

The preoccupations of poetry are the preoccupations of patients and their physicians—love, birth and death; pain, loss and suffering; grief, anger, elation and tranquility; and balance, harmony and rhythm.
        —J. M. Little, Mayo Clinic, 1993

Case One: The Young Woman

She visited me in my office one morning and I hardly recognized her. Five years later I cannot recall her name. However, her face and presence are still vivid in my memory. I was working in a medical clinic situated in a home for runaway youths. The young woman was in her late teens and at the time had been a patient of mine for several weeks. She was an attractive young woman, always neat and simply dressed, who wore little to no make-up or jewelry.

On that particular morning, however, she arrived at the office wearing a low-cut black blouse and tight black jeans. Around her neck she had a leather choker with a metal chain attached to a matching leather belt. She was wearing black lipstick and, when she took off her dark sunglasses, I could see that her eyes were ringed with dark eye shadow. Her appearance matched her mood—black and dark. We sat together for a while as I tried to gain some understanding of what was going on. She was very quiet and offered little information as to the reason for this sudden change in appearance.

When I had first started seeing her, I had reviewed her medical chart and learned that she had had a long history of recurrent episodes of abdominal pain and had been treated intermittently by numerous doctors. The episodes of abdominal pain had begun shortly after she had been physically assaulted when she was twelve years old. Over the next few years she had started having problems in school and eventually dropped out. She left home and subsequently ended up in this home for runaway youths.

After this particular visit when her appearance was so changed, we saw each other regularly over several weeks. I could find no physical evidence of illness, but it was quite apparent that emotionally she was deeply disturbed. After several more visits she eventually disclosed to me that a "close friend had died" in her arms and she was "mourning his death."

Our encounters were "simple ones" from a medical standpoint, but very challenging for me as a physician from a spiritual perspective. I learned how to truly listen to her story, not only to what was being said but, more important, to what was not being said. I had to be completely attentive to her presence. I had to empathize with this woman in black, keeping in mind that the young woman I had met just weeks before was still there, somewhere under the dark make-up, clothes, and chains. Both these "individuals" made up this young woman. It was my role as a caregiver to be nonjudgmental and accepting of her choices, offering her support and a sense of hope as she struggled through this difficult time.

In time, and with the assistance of other staff members, we were able to support and help her work through this dark period of grief and mourning. The young woman eventually returned to her former physical and emotional state. Several weeks later she came to visit me in the clinic. I was happily surprised to see her now dressed casually in jeans and a T-shirt. She just wanted to drop by the office to say "thanks!"

The good physician knows his patients through and through, and his knowledge is bought dearly. Time, sympathy and understanding must be lavishly dispensed, but the reward is to be found in that personal bond which forms the greatest satisfaction of the practice of medicine. One of the essential qualities of the clinician is interest in humanity, for the secret in the care of the patient is in caring for the patient.
—Dr. Francis Weld Peabody, Harvard, 1927

Case Two: Mr. & Mrs. S

I made my first home visit in November of 1991. It was one of many experiences that would change and shape my view of medicine and healing over the following years. Mr. and Mrs. S lived in a small, one-bedroom apartment and would be the first of many patients I would have the privilege of taking care of in their homes over the next several years. I had arrived early to the office that morning to meet the nurse and social worker who were to accompany me on the visit. Shortly after my arrival, the nurse insisted that we prepare to leave quickly. Mrs. S was on the bathroom floor and unable to get up.

We arrived at the couple's apartment and found Mrs. S, a heavy-set white woman, sitting unharmed on the bathroom floor. Mr. S was sitting in the living room by the window, smoking a cigarette. He was a thin, white man, not much taller than his wife. It was read-ily apparent that he was not capable of helping her rise from the floor. The apartment was dark and unkempt. The air was thick with the smell of cigarette smoke and the variety of odors that one encounters in a room that has not been cleaned for many months. The paint was peeling off the walls. There were half-filled pots of food on the stove. Piles of paper and boxes covered most of the floor space. As for the bathroom area, we immediately saw why Mrs. S would have fallen. The bathroom, like the rest of the apartment, was a dimly lit, small room with little space to move around easily. Inside the bathroom was a throw rug, half turned on itself, and the floor of the entrance to the bathroom was slightly higher than the floor of the rest of the apartment. Any of these factors could have caused the fall.

As is usually done on the first visit, we each made our initial eval-uation and I proceeded to obtain a full medical history and conduct a physical examination of the couple. Both appeared to be in stable health. Mrs. S in particular had no physical evidence of injury from her fall. We concluded that the fall was most likely due to environ-mental factors rather than medical ones. Over the next several visits, simple changes were implemented to improve the bathroom area and reduce the risk of future falls.

During one of our early visits to the couple, for some unknown reason they refused to let us into their apartment. We attempted for several minutes to talk to them through the door. We could hear them moving about inside the apartment and, though they were talking to each other, they would not respond to us. Finally, we heard Mr. S say "Ssh! Be quiet and maybe they'll go away!" We left shortly after that and returned to the office to determine our next course of action. This change in behavior and mistrust of the medical team was a surprise to us. We never determined the reason for their behavior but did eventually, with the help of an outside agency, re-establish a good working relationship with the couple.

In my visits over the next few years I learned a great deal about the couple. Mr. S had been born in Germany and was a Holocaust survivor. He had lost his first wife during the war in a German concentration camp. Believed not to be Jewish, he was sent to a relocation camp in England and eventually came to the United States. He met and married Mrs. S in 1945. Mrs. S was born in New York. She had worked for many years as a receptionist in a private medical office, while he owned a gas station across the street from their apartment. Since their retirement, the couple had found it increasingly difficult to get around and therefore rarely left their apartment. They had no children and only one close relative, a niece of Mrs. S's who periodically kept in contact with the couple. They found much comfort in each other's company and had a close relationship with their home attendant and eventually with our medical team.

On one particular occasion, I was asked to see the couple earlier than our scheduled visit because the home attendant had noticed that Mr. S appeared to be ill. We arrived at the apartment and found Mr. S in the bedroom instead of in his usual chair by the window. He was sitting up in the bed and very short of breath. After examining him, we felt it was necessary that he go to the emergency room for further evaluation and possible hospitalization. Mr. S initially refused to go. We had to spend some time with the couple, explaining the situation and why we felt hospitalization was necessary. He eventually agreed to go.

During his hospitalization, I visited Mr. S every day. His hospital course went well without any complications. The most difficult part of his hospitalization was being separated from his wife. Because of her physical limitations, Mrs. S was not able to travel to the hospital. After each of my visits, I called Mrs. S to inform her of her husband's progress, and to see how she was doing. When I mentioned this to

Mr. S one day he asked if I would give his wife a message: "Tell her I love her and will see her real soon."

After several days, Mr. S happily returned home to his wife. Their lives slowly returned back to normal with a few changes. We visited them often during those first several weeks after his hospitalization. Neither harbored any resentment toward the medical team for the imposed hospitalization. We soon resumed the usual routine of our visits, providing medical care and spending time with them, talking about the current events of their lives.

I learned much from these two remarkable people. Their initial mistrust of the medical team after our first few visits was a concern for us and, in subsequent visits, we tried to create a safe, secure environment in order to regain their trust and continue their medical care. Over time, we were eventually able to do that. I learned, from their example, how to listen attentively and speak openly from the heart, which was the language that they understood. They were a loving couple. Each one's presence nourished the other and in the end they both nourished me.

I made my last visit to the couple in the spring of 1994. Shortly after that, Mrs. S was diagnosed with cancer and passed away in December of that same year. After his wife's death, Mr. S's conditioned deteriorated and he died eleven months later on November 8, 1995, four years to the date of our first visit to their home.

I am the resurrection and the life. He who believes in me though he may die, shall live.
—*John 11:25*

Case Three: J.R.

J.R. had been a patient of mine for three years. He was a handsome man, meticulously well dressed and charming. He was also HIV positive. Because of his illness, he was extremely conscientious about keeping his medical clinic appointments with me until just before his thirty-seventh birthday.

The breathing problem had started four weeks before and, though normally he would come see me right away when he developed any problems, he chose not to this time because he had planned a huge birthday celebration and did not want to miss it. I found all this out from his mother at the hospital on the day he was admitted for pneumonia.

I visited J.R. over the next few days. The pneumonia was severe and we talked briefly about placing him on a respirator to help his breathing, which was growing exceedingly more labored and difficult. J.R. had made up his mind the year before, after numerous visits and lengthy discussions, that in the event of a serious illness he did not want to be placed on a respirator. And despite the increasing difficulty in breathing that he was experiencing, he remained firm on his decision.

On what was to be my last visit with J.R. (although I did not know it at that time) I asked how he was feeling. He looked directly into my eyes and said he was "fine." But he did have a question for me. After a brief pause and with complete attention he asked, "What is it going to feel like?" My mind started to race. What was he talking about? Again he asked, "What is it going to feel like . . . dying I mean?" I sat there—confused, numb, and speechless. I had not expected that question and had no answer for him. I looked into his eyes and in a soft, trembling voice, through my own tears, said, "I don't know."

I went home shaken and dazed. I felt an overwhelming sense of fear and helplessness because of my inability to answer his question. And my feelings of inadequacy and apparent failure prevented me from returning the next day to visit J.R. He died the next morning and my sense of fear and failure was further compounded by a sense of guilt and regret for not having been there with him in the end.

While I learned much from J.R. as his physician, his true impact on me was as much in his death as in his life. Over time, I worked through the feelings of failure and guilt. And years later I came to learn that his asking me what dying would feel like was not so much a question to be answered as an invitation to be accepted. It was an invitation to be intentionally present and attentive to this man at a most special time in his life. It was a time when what he needed most was a nourishing presence, full of hope and full of love.

My experience with J.R. was life-altering and transforming. My failure was not in being unable to answer his question. My failure was in not being there, with him, as a source of strength and comfort, to help and guide him through his illness. As a doctor I could no longer treat his disease, but I could be a healing presence for him during his transition from life into death. I have thought about J.R. countless times since then, especially when sitting with dying patients and friends. He has changed who I am and how I sit with my patients. His presence was a tremendous gift for me as a doctor, for he taught me how to be a healer even when "cure" is not possible.

Encounters with Patients

Modern medicine is firmly rooted in scientific method and practice. Yet, despite technological advances, people still seek alternative and unconventional therapies. It has been suggested that the reason for this may be that an important element is missing from the patient encounter with the medical profession, and that what is missing is attention, on the part of the practitioner to the patient's "unspoken" spiritual needs. Such needs, if not addressed, could play a role in the noncompliance of the patient regarding medical care, causing the person to seek unconventional treatments or, worse yet, no treatment at all.

There has also been a shift in the nature of the doctor-patient relationship. Today there exists a general sense of disconnection between the doctor and the patient in the encounter. Several reasons for this shift have been proposed. One is that the current scientific nature of medicine and the education and training of its practitioners fail to incorporate spirituality adequately. Others are that spirituality is understood as a "competing rather than complimentary world view" ("Spirituality as a Clinical Tool," 1998); some physicians feel that religion (spirituality) should be kept separate from medicine (science); there is little published research which supports the usefulness of spirituality as a clinical tool; it is assumed that the responsibility of caring for the patient's spiritual needs belongs to other disciplines, e.g., psychiatry, psychology, or religion; clinicians are unaware of their own spirituality or do not have strong beliefs regarding spirituality and therefore do not incorporate it into their clinical practice.

During the past several years however, change has occurred that may lead to a more holistic doctor-patient relationship. Dale Matthews, M.D. (cited in Marwick, 1995), writes: "There is at work an integration of medicine with religion, of spirituality with medical practice, the twin guardians of healing through the ages." There have been a growing number of areas within the medical field in which the assessment of the patient's spirituality and support of the patient's spiritual needs are being used as a clinical tool in the healing process (Byrd, 1988; "Spirituality as a Clinical Tool," 1998; World Health Organization, 1990). Levin and others (1997) note a relatively new area of research called the "epidemiology of religion." The medical literature contains an increasing number of systematic reviews and meta-analyses supporting the protective factor of spirituality in the promotion of health. And the concept that spirituality is an essential, not optional, component of patient care is also being incorporated into medical school education and curricula.

Authors have set guidelines for how to assess the spiritual needs of patients through direct assessment using various questionnaires and scales (King et al., 1995; Riley et al., 1998). However, there is also a spiritual dimension to the encounter between the doctor and patient. Braverman (1987) refers to this as the divine-human bond between the patient and the physician, or, more specifically, the patient's own faith in the physician. This spiritual dimension between the doctor and the patient is not easily spoken of, but rather experienced.

The concepts for this aspect of medical care are ill-defined at best. In the medical profession, such concepts are rarely addressed. Since what one does not know often elicits feelings of fear, helplessness, inadequacy, and failure (as was the case in my encounter with J.R. prior to his death), such feelings can become a stumbling block for the visitor and therefore a barrier to the healing process.

Bessinger (1993) believes that "if we as physicians are truly to offer a return to health and well-being to...patients, we must develop an appropriate concept and language for discussing such abstractions as 'spiritual emptiness' during a medical encounter."

I have learned through my own experience in caring for patients that there is a spiritual dimension in the doctor-patient encounter. And I have only begun to formulate several concepts that I believe, when incorporated in an encounter, can help actualize that "divine-human bond," fill the "spiritual emptiness," alleviate some of the feelings of fear and uncertainty, and create a spiritual dimension in which true healing can occur.

Communication, Connection, and Communion

When two or more people come together in an encounter, many factors (conscious and unconscious) come into play that determine whether or not a bond will form. The formation of such a bond is not only important but also necessary for healing to occur. Three things (3 C's) are necessary: communication, connection, and communion.

While much can be said about communication, I will focus on a few fundamental aspects: listening, speaking, and silence. We hear with our ears but we listen with our entire body. Listening means total and complete focus on what is being said, without external distractions (sounds and events going on around us) or internal distractions (wandering thoughts, prejudgments, or assessments). When we are truly listening, our bodies are relaxed and still and our minds are open. In this way we not only hear what is being said but we understand as well. Listening is hearing with understanding.

Just as listening is not the same as hearing, the same can be said of speaking and talking. They are different realities. Talking can be anything from mindless babble or irrelevant chatter to pleasant conversation or moving speeches. Too often people just reiterate what has already been said (especially if they are not "listening") or talk at the other person, instead of with them, without regard for their presence. Speaking, in this context, is the act of talking openly and honestly from the heart.

Silence is an important part of communication and is absolutely imperative if true listening and honest speaking are to take place. For it is in the silence of the listener that true understanding of what is being said can occur. And it is also this same silence in which those who are to speak can formulate what it is they wish to say and discern what is truly in their heart.

Connection occurs when two or more things or people come together. In the healing process, I think connection is a creative process for all those involved. I group the process into three categories: creating space, creating safety, and creating sacredness.

By *space* I mean mental and emotional as well as physical space. Mental space means being completely attentive and present to what is occurring in the encounter. Emotional space means opening one's heart to the other person. Once this space is created, there is a sense of openness in which there are no temporal boundaries and, as a visitor, one becomes a source of support and nourishment for the other person.

The visitor must create a safe place for the encounter. People must feel a sense of security and trust before they will open themselves up to others. Confidentiality and empathy on the part of the visitor are of paramount importance. He or she must act in a loving and compassionate way toward the other person.

Sacredness is a topic on which countless books have been written. Sacredness in the healing process involves intentionality, hope, and gratitude. Being intentional means having specific reasons for doing something and knowing what exactly it is that one is doing and why. Hope is an essential ingredient in the healing process. It provides energy to those who are suffering and is the seed of comfort in the healing process. Gratitude is a state of humility in which, aware of one's own limitations and lack of control, one is accepting of all that has and will occur. It too is a seed in the healing process, a seed from which peace is born.

When communication and connection have taken place, communion can then occur. Communion is that state of grace in which the Divine enters and healing occurs. At that moment there is a feeling of lightness and peacefulness for all those involved in the encounter, as all come together and exist in one presence. These moments are usually not long lasting, but they have a profound effect on all those involved.

Conclusion

The encounter between the physician and patient is a powerful clinical tool for healing. While the concepts I have outlined have come from my experiences with my own patients, I believe they can be incorporated by anyone who is involved in the healing process whenever and wherever people come together.

Those of us in the health care professions, however, must strive in this new millennium to put the "care" back into health care. We must bridge the gap between the art and science of medicine. And we must reawaken the interest in humanity that is the foundation of our calling as health care providers and healers, taking care of the physical, mental, and spiritual needs of our patients in our encounters with them, thus bringing them back to health and wholeness.

For Further Reading

Bessinger, Jr., C. D. (1993). "Reflections on 'Soul' and Medical Art." *The Journal of the South Carolina Medical Association,* December, 572–575.

Braverman, E. R. (1987). "The Religious Medical Model: Holy Medicine and the Behavior Inventory." *Southern Medical Journal, 80* (4): 415–420.

Byrd, R. C. (1988). "Positive Therapeutic Effects of Intercessory Prayer in a Coronary Care Unit Population." *Southern Medical Journal, 81* (7): 826–829.

King, M., Speck, P., & Thomas, A. (1995). "The Royal Free Interview for Religious and Spiritual Beliefs: Development and Standardization." *Psychological Medicine, 25:* 1125–1134.

Levin, J. S., Larson, D. B., & Pulchalski, C. M. (1997). "Religion and Spirituality in Medicine: Research and Education." *JAMA, 278* (9): 792–793.

Marwick, C. (1995). "Should Physicians Prescribe Prayer for Health? Spiritual Aspects of Well-being Considered." *JAMA, 273* (20): 1561–1562.

The New Jerusalem Bible (1985). New York: Doubleday.

Riley, B. B., Perna, R., Tate, D. G., Forchheimer, M., Anderson, C., & Luera, G. (1998). "Types of Spiritual Well-being among Persons with Chronic Illness: Their Relation to Various Forms of Quality of Life." *Archives of Physical Medicine and Rehabilitation, 79* (March): 258–264.

"Spirituality as a Clinical Tool: Care for the Homeless Mentally Ill" (1998). *Healing Hands,* A Publication of the HCH Clinician's Network, *2* (December): 1–3.

World Health Organization (1990). *Cancer Pain Relief and Palliative Care.* World Health Organization Technical Report Series 0804, pp. 50–51, 57.

APPENDIX

Guidelines for Incorporating Spirituality in an Encounter

- *Healing is the process of restoration, in which one is made healthy, whole, or sound of mind and body.*

- *Healing can occur in the experience of being with a patient when the spiritual needs of the patient are cared for.*

- *The concepts discussed in this chapter are listed below and can be utilized by any practitioner of healing.*

Communication: listening, speaking, silence

Connection: space, safety, sacredness

Communion: a healing presence who is . . .

H　Hopeful

E　Empathetic

A　Attentive

L　Loving

I　Intentional

N　Nourishing

G　Grateful

Health Issues for Visitors

Kathleen M. Duffy

Since most likely you're not a health care professional, it's important, before you visit someone who is sick, to realize how sickness affects people emotionally, spiritually, and physically. This knowledge will help alleviate various fears you may have when visiting. For example, you might be uncertain about how to approach someone with an infectious illness or an illness that is frightening or off-putting to a non-health care professional. Of concern also may be visiting a person who is in need of physical or emotional help you are not qualified to provide. These topics and others need to be addressed before you can be comfortable visiting.

It is important to remember that you should be viewing the person being visited as a "whole," with needs that are intertwined and usually cannot be separated. Be aware that as we empower each person to attain her or his optimal level of health, we are helping that person to become the person God wants her or him to be. St. Irenaeus tells us that the human being most fully alive is the one who is most like the God in whose image we have been created.

Effects of Illness

While individuals are unique in their response to illness, there are some guiding principles that are helpful to remember. A person's response to illness is contingent on multiple factors, including: the perceived seriousness of the illness, the person's past experience of illness either for him or herself or another, the body part involved in the ill-

115

ness and its meaning to the person, the amount of pain being experienced, and the perceived outcome of the illness, including the effect the illness will have on the person's various life roles. It is usually possible to identify specific emotions that are common reactions to illness.

Egocentricity

When someone becomes ill, that person often has difficulty focusing on anything outside of him or herself. There may be withdrawal from the "ordinary" pursuits of life, and a lack of interest in what is happening outside of the individual's own sphere of illness. Thus, the person who is sick may not want to hear your stories about the latest movie you have seen or who won the World Series, or even what the weather is like. This shift toward egocentricity (turning inward) is a defense mechanism and may be necessary in order to marshal emotional, physical, and spiritual resources to merely survive, or to get well. It is truly a means of self-preservation and not an act of rudeness or selfishness.

Anger and Depression

Illness engenders many emotions, not least among them anger and/or depression. There are many objects for the sick person's anger—anger at oneself, at the health care system, at the doctors or nurses, at the family, or at God. The ways anger, whether appropriate or not, is manifested may be myriad. Obvious manifestations may be irritability, frustration, or misdirected anger (e.g., kicking the dog instead of the doctor). Many hospitalized people will have complaints about the food, the "service," the temperature of the room, but never be able to name the true source of their anger. It's certainly true that hospital food is seldom gourmet quality, but it often becomes an acceptable outlet for anger—the food can't talk back!

For Christians, anger is sometimes viewed as "sinful," and anger at God as totally unacceptable. Yet feelings are neither "good" nor "bad," they merely are. It is what we do with these feelings and how we act on them that is important. Psychology has taught us that depression is usually the result of unexpressed or unacknowledged anger. It may result as a response to loss. For the sick person, this loss can take many forms, including loss of control over any or all parts of life, change in body image (I am no longer the lovely, healthy, unscathed all-American man or woman), changed role in life (I am no longer able to be mother/caretaker for my children), loss of work, loss of physical/mental abilities, or loss of meaning of life (if I cannot be a productive member of society, I am useless).

Guilt

When confronting the issue of guilt, we need to be aware of cultural and religious influences that dictate to us who we should be. As Americans, we should be young, work-oriented, and productive. As Christians, we tend to feel we should be stoic and uncomplaining. Perhaps this is a "hold-over" from the tradition that says we must have done something wrong or bad to bring about our current suffering. The sick, suffering person may feel at some level that he or she has brought on an illness—"I wouldn't be sick if I had been having regular check-ups," or "I wouldn't have cancer if I had been more careful about my diet."

It is helpful to have some understanding of what illness means to an individual. Most people do not see illness as a good. Indeed, it is not our Christian belief that illness or suffering in itself is good. It is not. However, suffering can be a means of transformation in our lives and in our faith. What does the person we are visiting feel about her or his suffering?

Anxiety

A very common emotion experienced by a person who is ill is that of anxiety. There are many reasons for anxiety—some of them realistic and some imagined, but to the person experiencing anxiety, all of them are very real. Among many other fears, anxiety-provoking fears may include: fear of pain, fear of death or dying, fear of abandonment, and fear of an uncertain future.

Suicide

The visitor should be aware that suicide among people who are ill and especially those who are elderly is always a possibility. Statistics from the Centers for Disease Control tell us that in the U.S. more people die from suicide than from homicide. Suicide rates increase with age and are highest among Americans aged sixty-five and older. Therefore, it is necessary that the visitor be aware of signs that may indicate that someone is suicidal. Some of these signs will be subtle and you will not be aware of them until you get to know the person better or until a family member tells you about them. Some things that may signal severe depression and suicide risk include:

- Deepening depression—People who are depressed usually exhibit some signs, such as a lack of interest in usual activities (e.g., an avid reader no longer picks up a book, or a mother cannot find joy in her children), sad affect, poor personal hygiene, social isolation, change in appetite, sleep disturbances (unable to get to sleep or waking up very early in the morning). Illness and other stressful events cause temporary depression in most people, but some people already suffer from a depressive illness, making them more vulnerable to severe depression and suicide.

- Final arrangements—A person begins to put her or his affairs in order, changes a will, gives away possessions, talks vaguely of going away.

- Sudden elevated mood—The person may suddenly appear less depressed after having made a decision to end life, as if a burden has been lifted.

- Pre-suicidal statements—Direct or indirect statements about suicide or death. People who make such statements must be taken seriously, even if they appear to be joking.

All of these signs warrant further action. One of the first things you want to do is directly ask the person, "Are you thinking of suicide?" Don't worry about invading someone's privacy—this is important, and may be life-saving. You also should ask, "Do you have a plan, a method, a means?" Is there access to something that would enable them to take their life—a weapon or pills? Listen to this person. Be respectful and caring. Do not make judgments.

If any of the above signs are present, *you must act*. Depending on the individual situation, this action may take the form of speaking with the person's family, referral to a mental health professional, or calling his or her doctor or therapist. Don't leave it up to the person to get help on his or her own. If you sense an urgency about the situation, call 911 or a hot line, or take the person to a crisis center, emergency room, the psychiatrist or family doctor. Do not leave the person alone. If as a visitor you are uncertain how to handle this problem, there should be a back-up person (program coordinator, advisor, pastoral person, etc.) you can contact. Remember, you would certainly intervene if the person you were visiting were having a heart attack. The suicidal impulse is just as deadly.

Practical Medical Considerations

When to Call for Emergency Assistance

Keeping in mind that the decision as to whether or not to seek medical assistance belongs to the person you are visiting or the family, it is helpful to have guidelines concerning signs or symptoms that would prompt you to strongly suggest emergency assistance (e.g., calling an ambulance or 911). Among these are:

– the person you are visiting becomes unresponsive

– the person is having severe difficulty breathing (breathing may be rapid and shallow/skin may be dusky, especially around the mouth)

– the person you are visiting has chest pain that persists for five minutes or more, or has taken three Nitroglycerin pills without relief, or the pain is accompanied by shortness of breath

– any uncontrolled bleeding

– any change in a person's mental status (e.g., the person

suddenly cannot remember where she or he is, becomes agitated or upset, or is having difficulty speaking).

It is generally better to err on the side of caution and call for assistance if there is any question that the person you are visiting seems acutely ill. Once the health care professionals arrive (and, of course, you would remain with the person until help arrives), they will take over and assess the situation.

Referrals

As a visitor, you are not expected to know everything! For this reason, it is a good idea to develop a list of resources that may be needed by people you visit. This would include community resources: health care (whether physical or mental), social services, nursing services, pastoral resources. Before making a referral, it is necessary to have the person's permission. You do not have the right to assume that the person you are visiting, or that person's family, needs or wants any of these services. Depending on the individual situation, it is usually best to provide the person or the family with the phone number of the requested referral and have them make the call, rather than calling yourself. This assures the person's privacy and forces him or her to take the initiative, thus more likely resulting in the person's keeping the appointment or following up as needed. You can only suggest and encourage.

The Visit

Before the Visit

Depending on the protocol of your organization or community, there should be initial telephone contact with the person to be visited. This will enable you to gather information and evaluate whether this person should be visited and by whom. When you as the visitor are given the name of the person to be visited, he or she should be expecting your call. When you telephone to make an appointment for the visit, you need to state your name clearly, who you are (e.g., "I am from the parish Partners in Healing"), and why you are visiting (e.g.,

"You asked to have someone from the parish visit you"). During this call it is important to get details, such as the exact address, apartment number, and any special instructions for entry (e.g., if you need to ring a neighbor's doorbell). Set a time for your visit and stick to it or notify the person to be visited if you are going to be late. Often people who are elderly or weak will sit by the door or the intercom and wait for you because they move slowly. Be considerate.

When visiting, it is imperative that you consider your own personal safety. Know where you are going and how to get there. Do not go alone if the area is unfamiliar or if you feel unsafe or uncomfortable. In apartment buildings, use elevators, not stairs. Have some form of identification with you and show it to the person you are visiting. You also may wish to let your coordinator know when and where you will be visiting.

Use of Universal Precautions

When visiting anyone who is ill, whether in the hospital or at home, you should be using "universal precautions." These precautions are meant to protect both you and the person you are visiting from contamination by organisms or infectious material. If you adhere to these precautions, there should be no anxiety about exposing yourself to any health risk. Universal precautions include these: (1) Wash your hands just before visiting, at the end of the visit, and after you come in contact with the other person directly (i.e., touching their skin). (2) Use gloves when coming into contact with body fluid (e.g., blood, sputum, urine). Since you are not the health care provider, you will generally not need gloves, because you will not normally be coming into contact with body fluids. Hand washing is the best defense against infection. (3) Dispose of any soiled objects (e.g., used tissues, bandages) in a sealed or tied plastic bag.

During the Visit

Although you are not the person's health care provider, you may be the only one who sees him or her at home. Therefore, you may be the one to offer assistance or appropriate referrals. It is helpful to be able to do some assessment of health and safety. Most of the information you gather will be done informally through ordinary conversation and observation. As you converse with the person, you will be establishing rapport as well as an attitude of trust (remember to stress that whatever you discuss will remain confidential). During this visit, obtaining the name and telephone number of a family member as well as the person's health care provider is important if the person is agreeable. Respect confidentiality. The person may decline to give you this information. However, if it is explained that it would be used only in case of emergency, the person may be more comfortable giving such information.

Before getting too far into the visit, attempt to find out what the person you are visiting expects from you. You might begin by explaining what you see as your role (e.g., a spiritual companion, someone to pray with or for the person, etc.). You may need to set limits by explaining what you are not there to do (e.g., give medical/nursing care, do errands, clean the house!). From the beginning, it is important to establish a common understanding of your role.

An essential aspect of your visit is respect for the individual you are visiting. Concretely, this means that you should not ask about the illness or surgery—if the person wants you to know, he or she will tell you without any prompting. Respect also means not judging— not judging the person's appearance, the state of the home, or the type of illness he or she has. Often people who are ill or elderly are unable to tend to their own hygiene as they once did and are also unable to clean or straighten up their house. Indeed, it is precisely these things that may prevent them from requesting a visit.

While visiting, you may be able to observe aspects of the environment (the home or apartment) that may evoke concerns about safety. Are there things that could be a danger or obstacle to the person's ability to walk safely around the home (e.g., loose flooring, scatter rugs, furniture with sharp edges blocking a pathway)? Are doorways or fire escapes blocked? Is there a working smoke detector? If the person is alone and at risk of falling or becoming ill and not being able to get to a phone, is he or she wearing some kind of personal alarm system? You may point out any safety hazards you notice and ask if you can assist in remedying them. Again, you cannot fix everything; you can only make suggestions.

Another area that involves safety is medications. Today many people are taking multiple medications and can become very confused concerning doses and times. You are not the health care provider (sound familiar?). You may remind someone to take medication and even hand him or her a pill bottle if they ask, but you may not administer medication. This includes filling "medicine boxes" (usually plastic boxes with spaces for pills that are taken at different times and on different days). If the person you are visiting expresses confusion or lack of understanding about the medications, with the person's permission you may contact a family member or health care provider to assist him or her.

As you are visiting, you may become aware of other concerns for the person's safety and well-being. You may note whether this person seems able to care for her- or himself or for others (e.g., a parent who is not able to care adequately for the children). You may note whether the person's appearance is disheveled or dirty. You may also note whether he or she is able to obtain food, to shop, and to prepare meals. Some situations require intervention and need an immediate referral. This would be a time to speak to a responsible family member. During the course of your first visit, obtaining the name and telephone number of a family member as well as the person's health care provider is important. Of course, respecting confidentiality continues to apply and the person may decline to give you this information.

Conclusion

In case you have not caught on yet, *you are not the health care provider* during this visit! However, your caring, concern, and respect for the person you are visiting may impel you to assist in meeting physical and safety needs as well as emotional and spiritual needs. It is impossible to separate the spiritual person from the rest of the person. Having some knowledge of basic principles of care and understanding when and how to make referrals can contribute greatly to the quality of life of each person you visit. Relax and enjoy the company of the person you are visiting. You may be the highlight of his or her day!

For Further Reading

Glen, Genevieve, O.S.B., Kofler, Marilyn, S.P., & O'Connor, Kevin, eds. (1997). *Handbook for Ministers of Care.* Chicago: Liturgy Training Publications.

Lofgran, Elizabeth (1992). "What to Do if Someone You Know Becomes Suicidal." *Minnesota Depressive and Manic Depressive Association Newsletter,* March.

"Suicide in the United States" (1994). SA/VE CDC Statistic Page, National Center for Injury Prevention and Control.

APPENDIX

The Do's and Don'ts of Visiting

Do

    be yourself

    listen actively

    be respectful

    convey a caring, accepting attitude

    remember the spiritual focus of the visit

    observe any health or safety hazards

    refer person to needed resources

    sit within the person's line of vision

    speak clearly (but not loudly unless the person requests this)

    report suicidal thoughts or actions to an appropriate person/agency

    call for emergency assistance if person is acutely ill

    define your role

    tell the person when (if) you expect to re-visit

Don't

    give advice

    try to make it "all better"

    fill medicine boxes

    change dressings/bandages

    perform medical/nursing treatments

        – warm soaks

        – ice packs

        – massage

    visit if you are sick yourself

Role Plays

Divide participants into pairs and designate one as the visitor and one as the person being visited. Give the "person being visited" a print-out of the scenario. Allow adequate time for each pair to complete the exercise and then ask for comments from each pair.

Examples:

1. "I'm having lots of indigestion today. It's causing this heaviness in my chest. I drank some bicarbonate of soda, but it didn't help. Oh yes, I remember, my doctor gave me some little white pills to put under my tongue if my chest hurt. I'll take one (puts one under tongue). Hmm . . . it's still the same, I think I'm supposed to take two more (takes another, waits a few minutes, then takes a third). Well, they don't work. I think I'll lie down for a while. Could you come back another time?"

2. "I have to take so many pills. I take fifteen or twenty a day. Sometimes it's so confusing. I bought this medicine box so I could organize my medicines. Would you put my pills in the box—you know, in the box for the day and time I'm supposed to take them? It would be such a help to me."

3. "I've had this bandage on my arm since the doctor did my skin graft three days ago. It's getting very itchy. I have some new bandages, but it's difficult for me to change it by myself. Would you help me change it?"

Confidence and Confidentiality: The Ethics of Pastoral Visitation

Curtis W. Hart

What does it mean for a visitor to be in a confidential relationship with someone? What are the ethical principles that should guide the conduct of these relationships? What are the key ideas that training for visitation needs to impart in the area of ethics for any person undertaking this course of training?

While no one presentation can address these questions in any complete and exhaustive depth, this discussion of confidence and confidentiality is structured to provide essential principles and strategies helpful for responding to these issues. There is an old saying that applies here that "ethics are more caught than taught." All who participate in visitation become quickly aware that being a caregiver has to do with the spirit, the inner life, and ethical behavior reflects this inner core of value, belief, and experience. Further, all who participate in training for visitation need to reflect, for example, on the question of what it means to be a fiduciary, of how important it is to be a trustworthy person. This conversation provides a context that affirms the value of trust (being a fiduciary) in pastoral and indeed in all relationships. The objective, here as elsewhere, is to assist visitors in their understanding something of what theologian and ethicist H. Richard Niebuhr describes as an ethics of responsibility. Niebuhr believed that "fitting action, the one that fits into a total interaction as response and anticipation," stands at the center of every pastoral visit and every supervisory encounter.

It may not be productive to bring up this distinctly academic point with a group when it initially convenes for training. This perspective, however, inspires and is involved in the overall effort of sharing partnership in clinical knowledge and pastoral skill in visitation. To focus on this most basic idea, a variety of approaches are used: Bible study, role-play, mini-lecture, and group discussion. Not every participant interested in visiting will be equally at home with every approach, but there should be enough variety that trainees are bound to receive something worthwhile in the process.

It is always important to take time at the start of this or any other similar process to make a full set of introductions of seminar leader and participants. It is not certain whether participants, even if they have shared activities as part of a worshiping or other community for some time, may actually know or feel comfortable with each other. They certainly have little or no knowledge of the seminar leader doing the training. Warmth and openness are key to the start of building a healthy context for working together. In a one and a half hour session it is time well spent to devote at least ten or fifteen minutes to this activity.

Participants are generally surprised and, in fact, quite pleased to discover that the initial stage of their work together has to do with group Bible study. All persons are encouraged to share their insights. There needs to be a spirit of inclusiveness for all points of view. As is well known, simple, direct observations are often the most relevant to this form of learning based on sharing and reflection. The larger group breaks up into smaller units of six to ten, all of whom are asked to read aloud to one another and then quietly reflect upon the story of the healing of the paralytic in Mark 2:1–12. In this familiar story, a paralyzed man is lowered to the feet of Jesus to receive the gift of healing. Four men, presumably strangers, accomplish this sacred task by means of creating an opening in the roof of the crowded building where Jesus is preaching and then lowering the paralytic to him. Group members are asked to focus their response to the story by addressing these questions:

– What are the qualities that permit caregivers to help others get the help they need?

- How are we similar to the persons in the biblical story who lowered the paralytic to Jesus' feet?

- Have you ever "lowered" someone to receive help or been "lowered" yourself? What did this feel like?

These questions can be elaborated upon or added to by the contributions of group members. The responses of the small groups to these questions along with additional insights are then summarized and shared with the full group. Two major concerns that are central to pastoral ethics invariably arise: trust and responsibility. The various responses elicited in the exercise evolve into a collaborative effort at connecting what is "fitting" (useful, appropriate) in Niebuhr's sense to the act of care giving. These perceptions and ideas are gradually refined by the group leader and participants. Care giving is viewed religiously as a response to God's claim upon believers as a people of covenant and of baptism whose call is service to others. Group members may well add their own experiences and ideas about the role of trust and responsibility and what these values mean for them. The energy and interest stimulated in this segment of the session are typically sustained for the remainder of the group's time together. Thus, this activity is a crucial building block for success.

Once the larger group has finished recording its observations and reflects upon them, they are ready to proceed directly to an encounter with the issues of confidence and confidentiality. For purposes of definition, it is helpful to view confidence in a pastoral sense here in the terms articulated by Craig L. Nessan as "*implicit confidence* where material is shared with the caregiver based on an implicit understanding of the pastoral office without an explicit verbal agreement regarding confidentiality." This definition is useful in that it suggests that when one is visited by a representative of the parish church or other organization, it is assumed that trust and confidence will characterize the encounter.

At this juncture the group leader spends time emphasizing the importance of maintaining clear boundaries of confidentiality in the care-giving relationship. Put simply, visiting the ill requires that communication with fellow congregants and others should be treated with the utmost care and respect. Particular attention is paid to the problem of how to handle a person who brings up problematic material (e.g., marital infidelities, addiction) that is clearly beyond the authority or expertise of the visitor. At this point, referral is recommended in words that go something like the following, "You know, what you have shared with me sounds very difficult for you. I appreciate your being able to tell me. However, our pastor is really in a better position to help you than I am. How about if we call him together?" or "How would you feel about calling him yourself?" These and other similar approaches are listed and evaluated for clarity of expression and to test the degree to which they conform to what we are calling the ethics of responsibility.

Also important is the recognition that visitors may very well experience unpleasant sights, smells, or sounds in the role of visitor. Here it is well to maintain an attitude of what the famous physician, William Osler, called "*aequanimitas,* or seeming imperturbability and visible trustworthiness in the face of difficult circumstances." Practically speaking, this means that the visitor needs to think carefully about what he or she is saying and be aware about what the sick person may really need from the visitor. The best approach is to focus on the feelings of the person being visited and show real interest and concern in his or her world, all the while maintaining a presence filled with what Osler called "ever tender charity." Osler, the great physician, had a refined and powerful understanding of what *aequanimitas* could mean in helping relationships. It is an idea that can be helpfully carried into the art and act of visitation.

Further, participants are made aware of what in clinical ethics language is known as the principle of *beneficence/non-maleficence* or *"help and do no harm."* It is introduced as a principle useful in illuminating alternative courses of action and in clarifying a balance of benefits and burdens in response to tense situations. Simple examples may be very helpful in illustrating this point. Dialogue is productive for a variety of reasons. Most important, participants by and large possess little or no clear understanding or practical experience useful in sorting out the ways of communicating care and concern for others. At the very least, this brief conversation alerts them to the fact that these concerns are possible topics for follow-up supervisory sessions or for a follow-up discussion group.

Likewise, it is of importance to recognize *"autonomy or respect for persons,"* as the ethicist James Childress calls it, as yet another important principle for application in visitor contacts. For example, the group may discuss the importance of empathic listening as a foundation of trust that makes respect for persons a possibility. The group leader may offer an illustration of what happens when a visitor chooses to offer a personal opinion: "Well, the house is a mess... I guess no one really cares about you, do they... I wouldn't take it myself... Why don't you call so-and-so and tell them to come?" These sorts of expressions inhibit or negate potential for trust and confidence. Beyond these simple illustrations it may be helpful to ask if anyone in the group has seen this dynamic or experienced it directly. Invariably, someone can add a helpful illustration of when his or her feelings were neglected or trampled upon. These responses may then well be followed by the obvious question from the leader, "And how did that make *you* feel?" Sharing of personal experience is always a relevant way of making ethical principles and concepts come alive and make greater sense to participants.

The important issue of what it means to be a *fiduciary* is then advanced as a means of defining what it means to be a trustworthy person in the visitor's role. Because there has been previous focus on the "Person of the Caregiver," participants are in a position to grasp the implications of what it means *for them* to be *fiduciaries,* agents of trust and dependability. The take-home message from this section of the group process and discussion is as complicated and grand as it is simple and altogether basic: trust transforms visitors even as it stands as a pillar upon which any genuine caring relationship is founded. We are affirmed in our own personhood by our interest in and caring for others. It is by giving and receiving in trustful ways that our own lives of faith are deepened and enriched. Virtually all participants appear to comprehend this essential idea even as they are encouraged to recognize it as a dynamic in helping relationships.

Training for visitation should emphasize practical considerations with regard to dialogue and discussion of liability issues insofar as care giving is concerned. Effective training for visitation always emphasizes that the responsibility of the caregiver is that of facilitating and listening and not the giving of advice. Would-be visitors are advised not to give medical or other recommendations, but instead ask those who make the inquiry to speak again to their own physician or responsible party. What is at issue is very often inadequate communication or the timely need to review medication or course of treatment. New visitors are warned also to be careful in choosing what physical interventions they make and to undertake only those activities for which they have received clearance or instruction. The simple rule here is that if one is not sure what to do or if one feels uncomfortable, then one should look for instruction or advice from a supervisor or those in charge of the day-to-day care of the person being visited. Beyond the most simple of acts (lifting up a pillow or getting a glass of water, for example), referral is suggested as the strategy of choice. Second, the group leader reviews issues and entertains questions regarding insurance coverage for those engaged in a visitation program. It is suggested that knowledgeable individuals review current coverage and, if the visitation is being done as part of a program in a local church, that there be a consultation with the church's carrier or with knowledgeable individuals in the congregation's larger religious body (e.g., diocese, synod, association). Specialists in the field are best equipped to have the most up-to-date knowledge and expertise in the area of liability. By sharing themselves, they, too, become partners in the helping of others.

Group learning becomes more active, animated, and interactive as the participants take part in, observe, and comment upon a structured role-play. One of the group participants is asked to play a visitor who encounters a difficult situation at coffee hour after church. There he or she confronts a less than well-behaved fellow congregant (dubbed "Snively Whiplash, Esq." for mild comic effect) played by the group leader who asks a rapid series of questions: "What is this visitation program, anyway? . . . Is it some special group that is friends or aides to the pastor? . . . How did you get chosen? . . . And by the way, I heard you visited Mrs. J., an old friend of mine. How do you think she's doing? I just want to help here."

Mr. Whiplash is portrayed as the worst nightmare of anyone who has ever been "pumped" for information in a social situation. Is Whiplash truly concerned about Mrs. J. in spite of his inquisitorial demeanor? Are you obligated to tell him about the visitation program, Mrs. J., or anything else for that matter? What is the responsible course of action? What is "fitting" to say or do here? Invariably, all participants identify with the plight of the visitor. They want to be fair with Whiplash and hope that he is not a crass interlocutor or manipulator. And yet, on the other hand, they feel duty bound to protect the privacy and autonomy of Mrs. J. while maintaining the integrity of the visitation program.

The training group is now encouraged to cast about for ways of handling this difficult individual. The themes of boundaries, confidentiality, and setting limits emerge once more in the context of constructing an attitude and implementing a strategy designed to meet Whiplash where he is. With only slight encouragement, participants practice responding to Whiplash and the results can be summarized as follows: "This is a group that helps the pastor in visitation. If you want to learn more, I suggest you speak to him directly...Would you like to see a brochure about the program?...I can't speak with you about my visit with Mrs. J. more than to say that, yes, I went to see her. If you have a special reason for knowing anything about her, you need to speak with our pastor about this, too." Care and firmness must govern the interchange with Whiplash. He, like others in need of help, should be listened to both critically and empathetically.

Discussion here revolves around the need to be prepared to respond in a non-judgmental way to what is assumed to be Whiplash's coercive or baiting behavior. It is important to note that the role of the pastor or overall supervisor is crucial for success. Group members should have a realistic expectation that they can depend on their leader for support and direction. Support of this sort is necessary for the group to maintain coherence and strength. It is also very useful to have a suitable brochure available that accurately describes the origins and purposes of the visitors' group.

Finally, the discussion demonstrates another obvious reason for having a regular follow-up group for supervision to review encounters such as this one or others of a less problematic nature. It is important to emphasize here that all persons engaged in helping relationships profit from working through perplexing or problematic encounters with the help of experts and peers. No one is perfect. There is always room for support and feedback to maintain interest and effectiveness. Without review of this sort, visitors can be left with ongoing doubts or questions that may inhibit the fulfillment derived from caring for others.

It is always valuable to leave adequate time for wrap-up to review the major themes of the session. Time should be spent with any participant who appears puzzled or uncertain about what has been discussed. While the group leader need only provide a summary of the session, certainly there should be opportunity to share outstanding issues and the door must be left open to identify issues for continuing exploration. The process of training is open, not closed. By learning together in this way, the group leader and members are more trusting and respecting of themselves and each other. They have come to "live" the ethics of confidence and confidentiality, not merely talk about them. A training session or event may end with a prayer and silent meditation shared by the leader and group members as together they lift up their learning as valuable not only for visiting but for many other areas of life as well.

References

Childress, James F. (1982). *Paternalism in Health Care.* New York: Oxford, 55–76.

Nessan, Craig L., Th.D. (1998). "Confidentiality: Sacred Trust and Ethical Quagmire." *Journal of Pastoral Care, 52* (4): 356.

Niebuhr, H. Richard (1963). *The Responsible Self: An Essay in Christian Moral Philosophy.* New York, Evanston, and London: Harper & Row, 61.

Osler, William (1906). "Aequanimitas," in *Aequanimitas, with Other Addresses to Medical Students, Nurses and Practitioners of Medicine,* 3rd ed. (pp. 5–8). New York: McGraw-Hill.

For Further Reading

Bush, John C., & Tiemann, William Harold (1989*). The Right to Silence: Privileged Clergy Communication and the Law.* Nashville: Abingdon.

Childress, James F. (1982). *Paternalism in Health Care.* New York: Oxford.

Lebacz, Karen (1985). *Professional Ethics and Paradox.* Nashville: Abingdon.

Nessan, Craig L., Th.D. (1998). "Confidentiality: Sacred Trust and Ethical Quagmire." *Journal of Pastoral Care, 52* (4): 349–357.

Niebuhr, H. Richard (1963). *The Responsible Self: An Essay in Christian Moral Philosophy.* New York, Evanston, and London: Harper & Row.

Sulmasy, Daniel P., O.F.M., M.D. (1997). *The Healer's Calling.* Mahwah, N.J.: Paulist Press.

PART III
Supporting Visitation Programs

Practical Steps
to Developing Effective Volunteers

Patricia Cusack, O.P.

A History of Organized Volunteerism

The journey from barn-raising to helping at Ground Zero covers 350 years of Americans volunteering in increasingly organized ways. We are a country of volunteers, as the following examples show: the Revolutionary War was won through organized volunteers; the anti-slavery movement and the Underground Railroad included thousands of volunteers working for the cause; the New York Children's Aid Society was founded in 1853 to place homeless children in foster homes; Clara Barton's devotion started the American Red Cross in 1881; Big Brothers/Sisters of America have been mentoring needy youth since 1904; beginning in 1956, thousands of Jesuit volunteers committed themselves to working with the poor to improve their lives; the fifties and sixties saw a huge collective impact of volunteerism over civil rights; President John F. Kennedy ignited a whole generation of volunteers in the Peace Corps, now celebrating its fortieth anniversary; Americorps, our domestic Peace Corps, engages more than fifty thousand Americans in volunteer service each year; Habitat for Humanity, founded in 1976, has collaborated in building over one hundred thousand homes worldwide with volunteer assistance; and, today, AIDS organizations as well as a wide array of other issue-oriented groups increasingly rely on the work of volunteers. Indeed, from colonial times until the present, nearly every facet of

139

American life has been impacted by the work of volunteers. Given the impact of the advanced technology on all aspects of life, it is imperative that organizations, large and small, support volunteer initiatives with appropriate resources.

Recruiting and Supporting Volunteers

There are many ways to volunteer, in both formal and informal settings, and there is no exact prescription for organizing an infrastructure that will fit the practical needs for every context. If you are beginning the initial plans for recruiting volunteers in a not-for-profit religious setting, such as a parish or congregation, then the following practical steps are recommended.

Organize a Committee of Six to Eight People to Develop and Implement a Plan of Action

It is important to hand-select people who will be committed to the concepts that you are attempting to promote. If it is possible to recruit professionally qualified committee members, then do so. Keep in mind, however, that a well-balanced committee, in terms of the ability to offer time and particular talents, is essential to the successful implementation of the plan. Be open to the fact that individuals without professional experience are often the best contributors.

Look for people who have time to attend four to five meetings within a three-month period. Each meeting should last approximately two hours. It is strongly suggested that committee members have organizational skills, the ability to be team players, and above all, passion for the cause.

Usually, people who are interested in serving those who are ill, those grieving because of a loss, or those homebound because of incapacitation are individuals who are familiar with this kind of suffering from previous experiences with family and friends. Since finding the time to give to committee work will undoubtedly be a concern, suggest to members during the first meeting that a timeline be established. If committee members are carefully chosen, developing and implementing an effective plan of action should be accomplished in about ten hours. And, if they understand what is being asked of them, they will be more inclined to offer their best to the committee. It is wise to consider the possibility of committee members piloting the program with a small group of volunteers in order to work out the wrinkles before actually launching the program in a more comprehensive way.

Develop a Timeline and Organize Subcommittees

Before a timeline can be developed, it is critical that you share your ideas for starting a parish-based program with the people you have invited to join the committee. Obviously, a well-planned first meeting, with a structured agenda, will bring about the best results. It is assumed that a staff member has granted permission for the project and, in an ideal situation, will play an active role as a committee member. Ask participants to respond to your ideas and, of course, invite them to make suggestions. Once the committee understands the basics of the short- and long-range plans, it is time to move on to the next topic: establishing the timeline.

In discussing with committee members the practicalities of the timeline, be sure to consider the essential aspects of your plan of action. In other words, determine together how long it will take the committee to complete the various projects that are in the plan. The timeline must be reasonable enough to be managed well. It is best to allocate ample time for the completion of the various tasks rather than to be unprepared to implement the launching of the program because of time constraints. Finally, organize appropriate subcommittees to expedite the plan and encourage committee members to sign up for work that they find enjoyable.

What, then, are the basics of the overall plan of action beyond organizing a committee of planners and a well-developed timeline? The following topics must be addressed by the committee and are essential to the fulfillment of a successful outcome: (1) writing a volunteer job description; (2) determining how to recruit volunteers; (3) organizing training; (4) discussing the process for supervision and evaluation; and (5) sustaining volunteers.

Write a Job Description

Since the committee will have spent a reasonable amount of time discussing the details of the long-range plan, putting together a job description should be a manageable task. A two-hour session, facilitated by a leader, is recommended. During this time, ask committee members to list the basic tasks involved in a parish-based program that trains volunteers to serve those who are ill, grieving because of a loss, or homebound because of incapacitation. The following topics should be considered: (1) specific tasks that will be performed; (2) competencies that are required in order to perform the tasks effectively; (3) relevant information about the training design; and (4) an explanation of the support system which will be made available to volunteers. A prerequisite of a well-defined job description is that it clarify for potential volunteers what exactly is being asked of them. It is also advisable to list basic qualifications that would be desirable, i.e., age-specific competencies, life experience, and education from both formal and informal learning environments. While it is assumed that most potential volunteers are trainable, clarifying basic qualification characteristics can only help the recruiting process.

Recruiting Volunteers

It is important to be clear about the process for the recruitment of volunteers. Once a succinct and detailed job description has been written by committee members, it is recommended that it be advertised in the parish bulletin and/or newsletter. In order to narrow the pool of volunteer candidates, at least for the initial pilot program, presenting a job description that defines expectations of competencies and tasks will appeal to parishioners who feel they need a better understanding of what the job involves. Those who feel that they are not quite ready to participate will probably refrain from requesting an interview. Establishing reasonable expectations is most important during a pilot program because the goal is to achieve success by learning about what works as well as what needs to be modified. If too many volunteer candidates come forth initially, then the committee will find it cumbersome to manage the screening/interviewing process.

The next step is to organize the details of the screening/interviewing process. A non-threatening discussion between the interviewer and the interested parishioner will achieve the best result. The job description can be used as a basis for a stimulating conversation, since both parties are attempting to determine whether there is a "good fit." It is strongly recommended that candidates be interviewed by a team of two committee members. In the end, through the collaborative efforts of the committee, good decisions will be made regarding parishioners who will participate in the pilot program.

Training Volunteers

The best people to provide training for the initial cadre of volunteers are the committee members who have been actively involved in the planning process. In an ideal situation, however, an outside team of trainers would be available to any parish desiring to initiate a program of this nature. This is an effective way to ensure that volunteers will receive high quality training from trainers whose main objective is to enable as many parishes as possible to participate in this well-designed program.

Assessing the talents of committee members will serve to determine who is most suitable to provide necessary training. Recommended topics include: (1) social/interpersonal skills; (2) listening skills; (3) empathy and compassion; (4) spirituality issues; (5) understanding boundaries; (6) effective communication; and (7) legal issues.

The training should involve a series of sessions spanning several consecutive weeks. It is critical that volunteers be expected to attend the entire series and, upon completion of the program, engage in a critique of what was learned from the training. The critique is most effective if it is done in collaboration with the committee members who provided the training. If desired, organizing a guided group discussion around topics of concern is also a way to enable participants to talk about what they gained from the experience.

In the event that some participants feel that more training is needed in a certain area, as a result of either the one-on-one critiques or the guided group discussion, then committee members can accommodate them by setting up individual and/or small group sessions to further explore their concerns. Enabling volunteers to feel as prepared as possible will only strengthen the quality of the pilot program.

Assuming that the pilot program has been successful, a solid model is ready for implementation. Thus, the committee can begin to discuss when to launch the program. At this important juncture, it is critical to consider the possibility of inviting a talented parishioner, perhaps a committee member, to assume the role of coordinator.

Supervising and Evaluating Volunteers

Among the many responsibilities of the program's coordinator is that of ensuring that volunteers are supervised and evaluated. An effective way to provide non-threatening supervision is to build a buddy system. Initially, committee members would serve as buddies to the volunteers who participated in the pilot program. Once a strong cohort of trained volunteers is available to the parish at large, those wishing to supervise new volunteers should be asked to submit their names to the parish's program coordinator. Naturally, only those with experience in the program would be eligible for the role of supervisor.

Supervision entails providing formal or informal opportunities to speak with volunteers about their experiences as they attempt to reach out to parishioners in need. The education they received from the training, coupled with their own talents from life and work experience, will certainly enable them to feel prepared and comfortable with their ministry. Ultimately, supervision and evaluation intertwine and must occur on an ongoing basis and with a tremendous amount of respect for volunteers. If volunteers feel threatened by supervisors, they will undoubtedly be unable to do their best work for the parishioners they are visiting. The purpose of supervision and evaluation is to give volunteers an arena in which to ask questions, share stories, express concerns, and, more important, receive affirmation. A formal evaluation, involving written documentation, is not at all recommended. Remember that volunteers are most often well-intentioned individuals who are generous enough to leave their homes to bring good will to others.

It is recommended that supervisors be flexible about the style and context for supervision. Much can be shared and accomplished over a cup of coffee in terms of just listening to volunteers talk about their experiences of visiting the homebound. Alternatively, some people feel comfortable in a more structured context, such as an office setting. If a supervisor senses that formality is desired, then it is recommended that the volunteer's wishes be accommodated.

While it's best to evaluate volunteers informally by staying in close communication with them, especially during the first few weeks, it is also important to focus on the key elements of the job description. The job description was carefully written so that volunteers and supervisors would have a solid basis for understanding how to provide appropriate support to parishioners. The evaluation process, on the other hand, reminds volunteers that the ministry is important enough to be monitored and that there is always room for improvement and growth.

Volunteers in Action: Partners in Healing

The importance of putting time, energy, and financial resources into training volunteers and ministering to the homebound cannot be overestimated. Properly trained volunteers will provide the foundation for a life-giving program designed to alleviate emotional, spiritual, and psychological pain by making home visits to people who are suffering.

Beverly Musgrave, president and founder of Partners in Healing Inc., emphasizes the importance of providing training for parishioners who volunteer to support the healing process by providing pastoral care for the ill and homebound. The primary goal of Partners in Healing is to build a cadre of trained caregivers, within the context of a parish setting, who will work collaboratively with faith communities, educational facilities, community organizations, and health care systems in order to minister effectively to those in need.

Common Ground:
The Importance of Group Support
for Visitors

Elizabeth A. Baker

What Is a Visitor?

When I was sixteen, I discovered how important a visitor can be. I worked in a nursing home for older people who were no longer able to care for themselves but not so ill that they needed to be hospitalized. As a nurses' aide I was responsible for the daily bathing, feeding, and exercise of seven elderly people. In this basic caretaking job, I learned that through supportive relationships the spirit can still soar even when the body is weak.

One room on my floor housed two men, Frank and Charlie. Both of these gentlemen had Parkinson's disease, and they had entered the nursing home at approximately the same time. When I met them, Frank had not seen any member of his family for two years. He had not been visited by old friends or by members of his church. He seemed virtually friendless. By the time I began working at the home, he was barely alive. Although not in a coma, Frank appeared to be completely unaware of the presence of others.

Charlie, his roommate, had a stream of visitors. Old friends from his business days, family acquaintances, members of his synagogue, and endless relatives found time to drop by and be with him. His visitors were interested in him, and they showed their interest—both to him and to those of us in charge of taking care of him. I vividly recall his nephew questioning me about his diet, only to have Charlie inform him happily that I had snuck in some ice cream for him the night before! (Pistachio was his favorite.)

Though the progression of the disease was equally relentless in both Charlie and Frank, Charlie's spirit was buoyant. In the end, he lived not only longer than Frank, he lived better. While Frank was curled in his bed, not speaking or moving, Charlie insisted on getting up every morning in order to be showered, shaved, and dressed—always wearing his red tie—before visitors began to arrive at eleven. He had a new joke from the Johnny Carson show he had watched the night before to tell his nephew, and he sketched out an idea for a ring he was designing for his niece.

Both Charlie and Frank had sound medical attention. Both had the benefits of around-the-clock nursing care. But Charlie also had significant interactions with others; he not only knew them but he was known by them. Charlie's visitors kept his life going even as the Parkinson's eroded his strength.

How to Be a Visitor

Throughout this book you have been reading about various aspects of visitation—what you do when you visit someone. Before you *do* something, though, it is often helpful to know who you *are.* In your role as a visitor, what will you be for the people you visit? What happens when you are a visitor? In this book, when we say "visitors" we mean home visitors who supply comfort and companionship for people who have some special need. A visitor enters a stranger's life, offering eventually to become a caring and supportive friend. This is accomplished by listening, spending time with, praying with, and offering another person your support. Through your participation, a stranger can become an enriching friend to you, too. As a mutual attachment to each other develops, both of you will witness the unlimited support of God whose caring presence can reach out and sustain us all, even in the worst moments of our lives.

When there are crises in our lives—caused by illness or death, aging or changes in our lifestyle, natural disasters or catastrophes—

the support of a friend or confidante can help us get through. As I write this, my mother sits beside my father who has just suffered a heart attack. It would be almost impossible for her to visit him during the three short visiting times each day were it not for her friends who take turns driving her to the hospital. It would be almost impossible for her to make the many decisions concerning his care were it not for the seven children who take turns calling in to help her to decide. It would be almost impossible for the seven children to bear the difficulty of such decisions were it not for their partners, friends, and the ten grandchildren who offer their support. So too, as a home visitor, you can support and sustain another person who will originally see you as a stranger, but may later refer to you as "my dearest friend."

This book is designed to give the home visitor some knowledge of the visiting experience and the issues involved when one person extends the incredible hospitality of listening and supporting to another person. The later chapters focus on visiting skills such as empathy, and active listening techniques, issues related to death and dying, theological concerns, and health issues. The purpose of the book is to provide information and suggest techniques that can guide you in the many aspects of your home visiting.

The Simple Act of Visiting

This chapter concerns the visitor's experience when visiting and how the nurture and support of other visitors is the most essential ingredient in becoming a successful visitor. Visitors are "successful" when they are capable of continuing their visiting and stay attuned to the person they visit, regardless of the difficulties encountered.

Visiting may be accurately described as listening and being with another person. This sounds comparatively easy until it's attempted. It is actually very hard to hear someone else without almost instantly (and urgently) replying. It is even more difficult to "sit with" someone who is despairing and hopeless, grieving or feeling overwhelmed and not try to "fix it." To "listen to" someone, to "be with" someone, is powerful because it invites the person being visited into the experience that is closest to our earliest experience as children—the sense of being held. This "holding environment," as it was named by child psychiatrist D. W. Winnicott, allows a person to feel safe and to feel comforted. Every person needs to be held, especially in times of stress. It strengthens our ability to trust, to feel confident and safe, to feel loved. Visiting aims to recreate this "holding environment" by listening deeply and compassionately and by communicating caring and support. It's not an easy task, and it's essential that you not tackle it alone. Contrary to popular belief, visiting is not something that can be done well without support and guidance. Successful visitors work as a team with peers, supervisors, and colleagues who meet with them and provide ongoing support throughout the visiting process.

The Rewards and Risks of Being a Visitor

The sensitive and caring visitor resonates with the person being visited. Visitors often report that they feel the loneliness, pain, hopelessness, worry, or shame of the person they visit as powerfully as if it were their own. In fact, visitors will often find themselves absorbing the powerful outpouring of emotion that the one visited needs to unload on them. The visitor may feel overwhelmed and flooded by the pain and distress of the other.

The first visit I ever made was with an older woman who had just learned that the tremors she was experiencing were indeed signs of Parkinson's disease. I came bouncing into her dark apartment radiating the good health of a twenty-six-year-old seminary student. When I flourished the bouquet of flowers that I had brought with me to "cheer her up," she knocked them from my hand and actually growled at me to go away. Fortunately for both of us, I came back the next time empty-handed but more open-hearted.

People will have different degrees of readiness to receive and use help from the visitor. Their responses to the visitor may vary from warm acceptance ("I thank God that you are in my life. I look forward to our visits so much") to outright rejection ("How could God allow me to get this terrible cancer? And what do you know about it? You're young and healthy"). Visiting is a process. It involves making a relationship, and, like any relationship, it will change over time. Every visit will be different from the previous visit. Some visits will be satisfying and rewarding for both the ailing person and the visitor. Other visits may fill both of you with feelings of helplessness, frustration, or a sense of not being appreciated.

This is why visitors, when helping people in great distress, need an increase in the support they receive. They need encouragement to continue doing this difficult work. Visitors need understanding from others of the many conflicting emotions that may arise in them. They need a safe place to express their own complex feelings as they listen to other people's feelings. They need a consistent and trustworthy space in which to express their feelings, explore their reactions, and learn about the art of visiting by bringing accounts of their visits back to the group.

What Support Groups Must Provide for Visitors

Visitors need to participate and become members of a visitors' support group, one in which:

- the visitor has a place to express his or her own reactions and responses to being with a person in distress. For example, an older woman may feel guilty and depressed after visiting with a child dying from a brain tumor. She may believe that she should be the sick person, not the child. The support group can help her to express and re-examine her guilt.

- the visitor can receive supportive guidance about how to do the best job possible in visiting. For example, in many support groups, visitors talk about some of the "how-to's" of visiting: how to avoid giving advice; how to help the other (not the visitor) do the talking; how to know when to call for other help.

- the visitor can build an ongoing sense of community with fellow visitors. Community allows us to be known for who we are and to be appreciated for our particular gifts. In one support group, the visitors found themselves able to talk with each other and to share their own life stories and difficulties as well as those of the people they visited. Instead of this becoming a depressing exchange, many of the visitors found that they were better able to visit after they themselves had experienced a listening ear and an understanding heart.

The Importance of Support Groups for Visitors

A support group composed of fellow visitors provides powerful protective ingredients for the visitor. Groups help us to understand that we are not alone in our particular struggle. Many people are surprised to discover that once they reveal and seek responses to a problem, others empathize with them. Often this is because the others have had the same problem. When a visitor can receive support and understanding about a difficult feeling encountered in visiting (such as feeling angry with the person they are visiting) or a difficult situation (the visitor asks them to pick up mail and run errands), they can return to visiting strengthened by the encouragement of the support group. ("You mean you've often felt like you weren't helpful, too? You sometimes come away from visits feeling discouraged and inadequate?")

Groups can help us to develop creative responses that no single individual could produce alone. After discussing a situation in the visitors' support group, a visitor may come back to the person being visited with a new understanding of the situation, or with a new approach. For instance, the visitor can be helped to hear the deeper need behind the surface request. ("No, Mrs. Williams, I can't get your groceries. Maybe we could see about a home health aide. But it sounds like you really need more help around here. Will you tell me all about that?") They can, through their support group experience, learn to listen for a feeling that is almost being expressed and help the person they are visiting to talk more about it. ("I know, Mrs. Williams, that you want God to answer you. Usually, there is no easy answer to the question: 'Why?' And sometimes, we don't even want an answer. Sometimes, 'Why?' isn't even a question at all; it's a well-justified complaint. We are really crying out: 'Why me, God? Why, me?'")

The consistency of the group and the trust that deepens as the visitors meet regularly together build a mutual network of caring for all the support group members. It is easier to care for others when we feel cared for ourselves.

From Support Group to Community

As groups develop and mature, they can become more cooperative, helpful, nurturing, growth-promoting, and inspiring. In short, support groups for visitors can become soul food for each of their members. When a deep connection is forged over time through mutual sharing and caring and grows into an ongoing commitment of each group member for the other, community is born. How does a support group become a community? It involves spending time together, sharing our innermost selves, and developing mutual commitment to each other's health, well-being, and fulfillment.

The Development of Community over Time

What are the signs that a support group is becoming a community? Let's follow a support group of visitors and see the changes that take place as the group moves from its beginnings to the group's responses six months later.

In the Beginning

It is the first meeting of a visitors' support group and all of the members are first-time visitors. The group has a facilitator who has participated in her own visitors' support group for two years. The visitors have begun to see their people, and most have been on at least two visits.

The group sits in a circle and, as the session begins, Kay arrives late, looking flushed and close to tears. Other members of the group notice that she seems upset.

The facilitator of the group gently asks Kay if there is anything on her mind that she wants to share. At first, Kay talks about the subway and her many frustrations and difficulties in getting to the meeting. The facilitator and the group listen. Kay stops speaking and the room is silent.

The facilitator sums up Kay's feelings: "So, you're saying that you were so frustrated and annoyed because after a hard day at work it was even harder to get here?" Kay nods and relaxes a little at being heard. Group members begin to chat about the difficulties of travel for several minutes. Then the facilitator asks if there are other concerns, since beginning to visit can be stressful.

After a short silence, Kay speaks again and timidly reports that she also felt frustrated during a recent visit. She didn't know what to do. The person she was visiting had been diagnosed with terminal cancer and seemed to have no family or friends who visit him. After giving details of her efforts to ease his pain, Kay blurts out: "But the worst part was that he didn't feel helped by anything I did or said. He just slumped lower and lower in his chair and didn't even say goodbye when I left!"

At this, many group members murmur sympathetically. Some begin to offer Kay an extensive list of helpful suggestions. For instance, she is urged to ask about the person's cultural heritage and its impact on his illness. She is reminded to pray with the person she is visiting. Someone suggests that Kay visit more frequently. She is advised to bring along another friend or visitor to "liven things up."

Kay writes down the suggestions, but she still leaves the meeting looking worried.

The Support Group at Three Months

Three months later, Matthew brings to the group a situation similar to Kay's. Before the facilitator says a word, support group members notice that Matthew appears to be distressed. The group seems attuned to his worried expression and the agitated shifting of his posture.

This time it is the members of the visitors' support group who urge Matthew to talk about his frustration and his wish to be helpful to the person he's visiting. Matthew describes her as an overwhelmed grandmother with four young grandchildren in her charge. After listening with appreciation to the difficulties of the situation and the strong feelings Matthew has about this person's hardships, a group member asks: "Have you ever felt this way before?"

"I'll say I have!" Matthew answers. He seems relieved to be asked the question. "It's just like my family. My mother had to work, work, work just to keep body and soul together!"

Matthew goes on to talk of his early family life and how his visitation brings back memories for him. The other support group visitors are quietly supportive and sympathetic to him. As Matthew leaves the meeting, he looks more relaxed and says that remembering how he survived hardships in his childhood may help him encourage others now.

The Support Group at Six Months

At the six-month mark, the visitors' support group begins with much casual questioning even as the visitors enter the room. "How's your lady, Matthew? Has she finished the chemotherapy yet?" "Hi, Margaret, I checked on that housing application process. I'll tell you about it whenever you're ready." "Hey, Takesha, thanks for the phone call about the hospice. You rock, girl!"

Once again, the group encounters a member who is shaken and disturbed by a recent visit. The group easily notices that Ming seems especially quiet and depressed. Without prompting, the group begins to help Ming to share his reactions and responses to his dying parishioner. "I felt so helpless. She has so much life, but there's nothing I can do to stop her dying. She looks at me with such longing, and I know she wishes that something could be done. But it's hopeless. She has only a few weeks left."

In response, the group begins to recall how helpless and grief-stricken they felt when their own loved ones—parents, friends, colleagues—were dying. The group rallies to support Ming in several ways during the next week. Someone offers to call him before his next visit to strengthen him in facing his dying parishioner in spite of how painful it is to lose someone you love. Another offers to call him after his visit to help him process his feelings. All of the visitors remind Ming that this is a difficult time and that they care for him.

Change in the Visitors' Group

Over time, what changes most in a group is the comfort level. Group members come to the visitors' support group as strangers. In the first few meetings, some initial interest in each visitor is developed. As time alters first impressions and the facilitator helps the visitors to speak from their innermost selves, the group members can begin to develop deep connections to each other. Finally, as the visitors come to mutually trust and depend on their ongoing connection with each other, a commitment to each other's health, well-being, and success is solidified. We have reached a common ground on which we can stand. It has been forged by the mutual support and caring interest that each person of the group has for the others. The common ground has grown into a sacred space.

Patterns of Interaction

In the ideal support group, visitors share the talking time equally and help others to talk; they express what they are struggling with in their visits and open up easily about their thoughts and feelings. In reality, however, every group member is different. All enter the group with different levels of readiness for sharing their feelings, different abilities to share the talking time with others, different capacities to take in constructive criticism and feedback, and different degrees of willingness to reveal what their struggles actually are. In the beginning, almost all groups demonstrate certain patterns of interaction, such as monopolizing, withholding, and criticizing. This section will help you anticipate such patterns so that they can be more easily worked out in the support group meetings.

Taking up all the time. In the beginning of the group's life together, some group members may dominate the discussion and seek the group's constant attention, while others are more quiet and cautious. Sometimes the group seems quite comfortable allowing one or two visitors to do most of the talking for a while. However, as all the visitors become interested in talking, the group may become frustrated with a monopolizer. In these situations, a facilitator (or any visitor who can do so) can break up the monopoly by asking if other members would also like to talk.

Withholding. Often in the early sessions of the support group before feelings of safety and a sense of trust have developed, visitors may talk about their visits and about the people they are visiting while leaving out their own feelings from the discussion. Early group meetings, therefore, are characterized by helpful suggestions or superficial exchanges, but are devoid of lively and meaningful expressions of feeling. In these situations, visitors can expect that the group facilitator will let the visitors proceed at their own pace in terms of self-revelation, rather than pressuring group members to reveal more than they are comfortable with at the moment.

Criticizing. Another common situation arises when group members are inadvertently critical. In an attempt to "get it right," some group members may develop an initial pattern of criticizing other visitors' work. In these situations we often hear statements such as: "That's not really the best way to do that." "Do you *really* think that was helpful to your person?" "Why did you do it like that?"

When phrases like these appear, the group facilitator can ask group members if they are feeling criticized. Then it can be suggested, in the interest of developing safety and trust, that members practice speaking positively to each other.

These and other group situations that are commonly found in the initial month or two of the group are almost always worked out with the facilitator's help. As a result, the group is free to grow and the visitors are free to develop closer bonds that lead to an experience of community.

Community Begets More Community

Visitor support groups are a natural spin-off from the life to be found within the church and within church congregations. The Christian faith is concerned with the healing of the human spirit. The message of the New Testament is that all may receive God's love. Leaning on God's love, we are supported to live a fulfilling life fed by God's grace.

The first letter of John reminds us that love is felt and shared because we ourselves feel loved. "This is love. Not that we loved God, but that God first loved us. Beloved, if God so loved us, we also ought to love one another" (1 John 4:10–11).

This is where our faith and our communities of faith offer us sustenance. The parish setting brings us together into a community that shares worship, study, prayer, and outreach to others. We receive the message of God's love for us. Even more important, we feel the love of our brothers and sisters in Christ within our community.

It works the other way around as well. As we get support in our visitors' group, we feel the benefits of community. We learn how to be better listeners, better healers, and better supporters. We take that learning back into all the other significant places of our lives—our homes, our jobs, our schools, and especially our parishes.

"This is love." As the visitors experience the acceptance and support of their visitors' community, they will be empowered to go out from it able to learn, to listen, and to love.

Getting past the Fears

In any group, people reveal something about themselves as they work with the other group members. Participation in a visitors' support group requires members to reveal aspects of themselves to other people whose reactions cannot always be predicted or relied upon. Especially as visitors discuss their experiences with persons they are visiting, they may uncover feelings or remember experiences that are uncomfortable or difficult. Often visitors worry that their contributions to the group will be seen worthless, stupid, or crazy and leave them feeling ashamed. Sometimes, visitors report they expect to find only rejection or criticism from others in the group.

The experience in the visitors' support group varies for each member. How a visitor feels in the group may depend on the way in which each visitor perceives the group. For instance, if a visitor sees the group as a helpful, supportive gathering of people who respect each other's contributions, the visitor's rating of the group will likely be rosy. She or he will often report receiving positive feedback. Perhaps a visitor may have had previous experience in groups that were intolerant of differences or had rigid rules of conduct, such as might be found in certain schools or even in religious institutions. Such a visitor may walk into the first meeting of the support group and demand to know who's in charge and what will be required of the group members.

Initially, the past family life of all the visitors is a factor in how they see the group. A visitor who has come from a critical family, where nothing he or she did was right, may anticipate being criticized in the support group. If a visitor comes from a family where conflict was constantly erupting but never resolved, the visitor may fear fighting endless battles in the group. Visitors who have had the experience of achieving something in life only to have others say "But what about...?" may always be looking ahead to the next task. It's helpful if the visitors are told to expect this at the start and go on to explore important family relationships later on in the group when they feel safer. Visitors' support groups ideally strive to maximize the chances that members will not only learn to *do* something outside of the group but that they will also learn to *be* something inside the group. These experiences allow visitors to experience their own true needs, to forgive and be forgiven, to develop self-understanding, and to be accepting of others.

Guidelines When Setting Up Support Groups

In order to set up a positive and productive visitors' support group successfully, certain group dynamics must be put in place.

Visitors must feel reasonably at ease with each other. Ease in a group setting is largely accomplished by the facilitator and the visitors through the exercise of the art of listening. If there is a facilitator, he or she may set the standards by asking respectful questions, sharing a feeling, or inviting exploration of an idea. Attitude is everything, especially at the beginning. Visitors set the tone by accepting any feeling, concern, or fear that others express without punishing the person expressing them. If an interested but non-judgmental stance can be developed in the support group, the visitors can be reassured that their community will be a safe place for them to discuss their concerns, express their needs, and provide each other with an empathetic ear.

The visitors must develop mutual trust. This allows feelings and experiences that are often censored in other places to be expressed openly and appropriately. The facilitator may outline the purpose and the methods of the visitors' interactions with others at the very first meeting. An introduction to the formation of some "common ground" could be as follows:

Welcome to the visiting experience. Over the next several meetings of this support group, you will get some information and guidance about how to become a visitor. Even more important, you will be giving each other help on how to be caring and committed visitors—both within this group setting and outside of it, in the parish or in the wider community. In this group we will talk about topics that are of interest and concern to all of us. Everyone is encouraged to contribute her or his thoughts. You may feel scared or silly. You may think your ideas are unimportant, but they are not. You can never know beforehand how useful your ideas may be to someone in the group, and sharing them will enhance everyone's learning. At the same time, try to be sensitive to the other visitors. Give them a chance to speak, too. One of life's big discoveries is that people rarely *really* listen to each other. They interrupt or think about what *they* are going to say next. I will be helping you to really listen and to honestly respond to what you have heard. Listening, as you will soon discover in your visiting, is extremely powerful and it often turns out to be the most helpful thing even in the most difficult situations.

The visitors' group should be as congenial as possible with regard to their ways of expressing themselves and modes of interaction. If many of the visitors in a support group can agree on the unwritten rules of conduct in the group, the group can more easily build safety and trust among its members. For example, if visitors can agree that all honest, respectful expressions of feeling are welcomed in the group and all the visitors strive to follow this standard, the group's development is enhanced. Conversely, if some visitors want group members to speak only about positive or pleasant visits or are urging other visitors to always "look on the bright side of things," the support group can get bogged down when the inevitable variety of reactions to visiting begins to emerge.

The visitors' group should be as diverse as possible with regard to the visitors' "differences." Diversity in a group produces flexible strength and the ability to adapt to the changes that the group as a whole will undoubtedly experience. Different ages, cultures, life situations, and experiences enliven and enrich the visitors' understandings of the various ways in which healing can happen. Each person (in and outside of the group) is approached with the awareness that as we empower each person through empathetic listening, we are helping that person to become the whole person God wants him or her to be.

Conclusion

The visitors' support group is an essential part of the visiting process. Support groups are strongly recommended because visiting is one of life's incredibly powerful and radically transforming experiences —not only for the one visited but also for the visitor. As the visitors regularly return to the support group, bringing accounts of their visiting experiences with them, all the visitors are strengthened in their work. Being together deepens their connection to each other and to those they are visiting.

Visitors need some space where they may feel the love of God as it is communicated through others' active concern for them in order to meet the people they are visiting with the same loving connection. We have named this the common ground—the place visitors reach when they mutually trust each other and depend on their ongoing commitment to each other. By setting forth from this community of caring and support, visitors can enrich the lives of all they touch, including their own.

Visiting adds an invaluable dimension to life, both for the one visited and the visitor. Although it is not an easy commitment to keep, the rewards are often amazing. Visiting is energizing, heartening, liberating, and enlightening, all at the same time. It profoundly touches the soul and makes the spirit soar.

So, come along with all of us who strive to be healers in a less-than-perfect world. Take an amazing journey into another's life and discover new things about your own. Make an investment in yourself; become a visitor! Oh, and bring a friend.

For Further Reading

Dickoff, H., & Lakin, M. (1963). "Patients' Views of Group Psychotherapy: Retrospections and Interpretations." *International Journal of Group Psychotherapy.*

The Holy Bible: Revised Standard Version (1952). New York: Thomas Nelson & Sons.

Winnicott, D. W. (1965). *The Maturational Processes and the Facilitating Environment.* Madison, Conn.: International Universities Press.

Winnicott, D. W. (1975). *Through Paediatrics to Psycho-Analysis.* New York: Basic Books.

Yalom, I. D. (1970). *The Theory and Practice of Group Psychotherapy.* New York: Basic Books.

Critical Issues in the Development of a Pastoral Visitation Program

Michelle D. White

This chapter describes the development of a pastoral visitation ministry at a small Baptist church in Bedford Stuyvesant, Brooklyn New York, and looks at several critical factors in developing a faith-based pastoral visitation program in an urban African American community. Among these are using the Bible as a lens for analysis, the impact of the current health care crisis facing the urban poor across the United States, and the influence of African American culture on notions of illness and health. Finally, by sharing the successes and failures of the pastoral visitation team in one church community (one that may share characteristics with many others), other faith communities may be led to devise programs appropriate to their own situations.

Social Reality in Bedford Stuyvesant

The Universal Baptist Church, located in the historic African American community known as Bedford Stuyvesant, has existed as a community of believers for more than seventy years. A team of fifteen church members, including the pastor, received ten weeks of training in pastoral visitation from Partners in Healing. The team subsequently endeavored to refine and expand the pastoral visitation program to fit the needs of the church community of about 140,000 people. Bedford Stuyvesant is home to hard-working people who have successfully crafted lives for themselves and their families. The community boasts a rich worship history and a number of historic and influential churches. Beautiful, well-kept brownstone homes border many of the tree-lined streets of the community in spite of three decades of economic hardship.

Much of the community's character has been preserved although changes in the global and national economy have devastated the lives of many of the residents. Social and political forces arrayed against similar communities across the United States militate against individual success. Structural changes in the U.S. economy, the deliberate manufacture of chaos through the drug trade, a biased legal system, and an ineffectual educational system are pervasive features of current community life in spite of the community's grace-filled history. Forty-two percent of community residents hold jobs as managers, technicians, and professional workers; however, a nearly equivalent number are considered to be low-income. More than forty-five percent of the residents receive some form of government assistance. A health crisis exists, and it is clear that the church must not collaborate with the government's failure to provide for its citizens.

The incidence of HIV/AIDS, tuberculosis (which is on the increase), hypertension, and diabetes in this community is predictably and unacceptably high. It is simply a fact that African Americans nationwide are over-represented in all categories of serious diseases and in infant mortality rates as well. These conditions are repeated among all poor and marginalized groups in our country and are particularly devastating for women and children.

Recent and dramatic changes in the U.S. health care delivery system have contributed to and exacerbated this public health crisis. Shorter hospital stays, more complicated reporting policies for insurance claims, and an absence of any medical coverage have created a crisis for many members of the community. Children are most profoundly affected. In dealing with the critical changes that have taken place in the delivery of medical services in the low-income portion of the community, the local church must consider a new paradigm to address the healing and recovery needs of community members.

The African American church has historically concerned itself with a "love discourse" that forms its members into a bedrock for the communal profession and practice of love and the expression of mutual concern. This is, however, not exclusively an African American perspective; it is a Christian perspective. The "love discourse" tries to transcend socioeconomic differences in the community. The church has traditionally created a system of care that has made survival in each community possible. A collective redistribution of wealth occurs through the collection plate to meet the needs of those less fortunate in the community. Unfortunately, though, in spite of the best efforts of many of our community residents, the interaction of social, political, and race-based structures that systematically affect the poor in communities nationwide has created conditions in the lives of our people that churches must address in new and creative ways if we are to do what the Lord requires of us. It is our hope to integrate the pastoral visitation concept into the existing concept of traditional care and existing church structures.

The Case of Ms. Smith

Just what is this "love discourse" and how is it played out in this church community? The needs of the widows and children, according to scripture, are to be addressed by deacons. Deacons and deaconesses are responsible for assisting those who are unable to attend to certain issues for themselves. When church members are hospitalized or have suffered loss, they receive a visit from members of the diaconate. Such a visit will include prayer, a loving presence, and a listening ear.

When the "love discourse" meets the harsh realities of life in the urban setting, it is not essential to understand how the realities of globalization, restricted availability of health care, rising unemployment, welfare reform—conditions that are entirely beyond individual control—are manifested in human lives. What is important is to fully understand how ordinary church members who are prepared with specific training may better address the needs of those who suffer. Consider the case of Ms. Smith, a thirty-year-old mother of one daughter. After recent major surgery, she was hospitalized for fewer than five days and released to an apartment in a building controlled by drug dealers. Ms. Smith was unable to shop or cook for herself, a job that any deaconess would willingly assume. But what about the course of Ms. Smith's recovery? The deaconess as pastoral visitor will also recognize infection, should an infection develop. She will be aware of Ms. Smith's discharge plan, her prescribed medication, and guidelines for activity following surgery. The deaconess is not a doctor, simply an informed pastoral visitor. Should the deaconess recognize a problem, her responses may include a call to emergency medical services or a discussion with the trained health professional who supervises the entire visitation team.

As Ms. Smith struggles to recover from her health crisis, she must navigate a health care system dominated by managed care. Managed care has become an important aspect of marketplace health care provision if Medicaid is to control costs and allegedly improve access for the poor. Ms. Smith must therefore make an appointment to see a primary doctor, obtain a written referral, and finally see the appropriate specialist, who is most likely overwhelmed by the demand for care. A member of the visitation team, a social worker, will assist Ms. Smith in accessing additional care and pray with her during her ordeal.

Ms. Smith's situation may at one time have been an isolated case, but her situation is now common in my church community. This desperate health situation is compounded by the existing social conditions that are common life challenges in this community. Ms. Smith is victimized by a profit-driven medical system. As was true for the prophet Amos more than twenty-five hundred years ago, so it continues today. These are "they who trample the head of the poor into the dust of the earth, and push the afflicted out of the way" (Amos 2:7–8).

How can a pastoral care ministry help Ms. Smith? In each congregation there are many loving, caring individuals who desire to be the hands of Christ. There are women in my congregation who have met the challenge of addiction, struggled with homelessness, and raised children successfully in spite of serious life conditions. There are men who really see the needs of those around them. These are ordinary people who are used in extraordinary ways every day by a loving God. Caring individuals in every congregation can help to make recovery and re-integration into the community less difficult. There is in every church and in every community the potential for loving mutual support for those who are struggling with illness, addiction, and loss; there is in every congregation a cadre of people, of servants, who desire to use their skills and training to serve God's people in more specific and intentional ways. Visitors are willing to journey with Ms. Smith just as someone once journeyed with them. There are members of our congregations who desire to live out the words of Jesus found in Matthew 25:35–36: "...for I was hungry, and you gave me food, I was thirsty, and you gave me something to drink, I was a stranger, and you welcomed me, I was naked and you gave me clothing, I was sick and you took care of me, I was in prison and you visited me."

The Power of the African American Church

The coincidence of the medical/technical, sociopolitical concerns of the twenty-first century and the traditional transformative effects of African American worship combine to make the pastoral visitation team one of a number of viable means for addressing individual and community health in a faith context. Theorists have long understood the Black church's function as a therapeutic community. The traditions of my own faith community grow from strong ties to traditional African and Southern origins, and, while not all African American worship experiences are necessarily similar, there are commonalities that transcend socioeconomics, context, and denomination. It is in this worship context that expressions of anguish, disappointment, hope, and joy may all be legitimately and acceptably mixed with adoration of the Divine. African American worship is also remarkably similar in some ways to the pulsating beats, the pounding feet, and the ecstatic utterances of those who worship in many parts of Africa, the Caribbean, and the United States, and it is in this context that healing, both physical and psychological, occurs. It is in this context that faith is active, prayer is continuous, and miracles are expected.

In this shared and embodied speech of African American worship, spirits leap, hands fly up, and, by virtue of the shared suffering mixed with assurance, all leave knowing that we're all going to get home someday because God himself is made manifest. It is the heat of worship, the physicality of worship, the beat of worship, and the ecstasy of worship that encourage the Divine manifestation and make the miracle of continued life possible in spite of despair. This worship is mysteriously empowering. Ms. Smith can return to the world where the continuing and ever-evolving reality of inadequate health care and poverty exist but are subordinate to the Divine power that sustains her and is present with her in the members of the pastoral visitation team.

African American worship also grows from the promise of a collective "turning to God." In every worship experience, this faith collective, this family of believers, turns to God, each person with her or his specific lament, knowing and trusting that God will hear and deliver, just as God has always done. Ours is a God who "hears and answers prayers." Everyone knows that God sees what's going on and is keeping count of the offenses (Psalm 56). Even the children know that God is our refuge and our strength even in battles with municipal governments (Psalm 46). All are trusting that God will hear the needy (Psalm 69:34). All are trusting that just as YHWH promised to be with the children of Israel in all their wanderings, his same presence remains with marginalized people today.

It is our need and privilege to turn to God, to cry out to our Very Present Help (Psalm 46:1), and to *expect* deliverance. Joyful expectation is the culmination of communal purging and preparation for continued challenge in the personal lives of members of the worship community. This promise empowered the apostolic community of believers in the first century C.E.; it empowered our foreparents on this continent, and it still empowers African American believers today. We will go on knowing what the Hebrew prophets understood: none of this will change through human agency alone. God will act to redeem God's people. Every Sunday, we're "all in one place and on one accord" and in the position to receive the power and support of the worship community. Resurrection is celebrated, and the community is enabled to move with new hope into the future. This is the promise that a pastoral visitation team embodies.

How, then, does this African American or any worship community move from the ecstasy of worship to the depressing challenges of life? The answer can only be that there is no separation between the sacred and the secular. Every opportunity to visit and serve is an opportunity to stand with another on his or her "holy ground." Every opportunity is an act of worship where we are privileged to represent a loving God to each other. To maintain a separation between worship and service would mean death for many in my community. The crushing waves of despair that routinely confront Ms. Smith would completely overwhelm her without the assurance of God's presence working in and through each believer and every situation. Were it not for God's presence, we would certainly wither and die. Pastoral visitation ministry occurs and succeeds because of God and through God's Spirit working in each of our lives. This pastoral visitation ministry, by virtue of African American worship, history, and practice, is a ministry that is appropriate to the African American experience. It is one where the characteristics and understandings of the worship community underpin the program. It is therefore a ministry that is sensitive to people's needs in context, regardless of race, income, creed, or denomination.

It should not be assumed that because this pastoral visitation design worked well in one African American faith community, similar results will be achieved in other African American or marginalized and poor communities. Attention to local traditions and customs may be necessary in order to adapt and adopt the visitation paradigm. Although there are similarities in African American worship, due in part to the kinship of slave history, our variety in worship is probably just as important as the similarities. Yet even more important than similarities in historical experiences or varieties in worship is the commonality of social, economic, and structural realities faced by African American and other marginalized communities. These realities affect all of us as Americans, regardless of denomination, personal history, or worship tradition. The trained, skilled members of the pastoral visitation team seek to address these issues by accessing and using the power inherent in communities of faith.

If there is any possibility for hope in the life of Ms. Smith and the lives of so many others in our communities, hope must come from the one institution that has always been present in difficulty, the one institution Ms. Smith trusts to journey with her through these and future difficulties. The church is that institution, and we as pastoral visitors are the church.

Shared Perspective

In order to be more faithful to the African American perspective, this reflection must include perspectives from other African American faith communities. These voices include Pentecostal, Apostolic and AME views on illness as punishment, the church's responsibility to those who suffer, and the position of the pastor as a model for the delivery of pastoral care.

An important perspective on illness was shared with me by a minister from another denomination. She recalled her childhood experiences with illness among members of the church family and her childhood understanding that it is certainly possible to be faithful to God, to pray fervently, to have others pray fervently and regularly for you, and to still be sick. It is also important for members of the community to know that prayer or "the laying on of hands" might not necessarily confer the expected healing in the desired ways. It is important for members of the church community to know how personal needs and desires can be projected onto another person, even in the ministers' zeal to serve in this pastoral way. We are all subject at times to attitudes that attribute illness to sin, judgment, and a failure to "pray right."

The Lord Jesus corrected this misunderstanding in his disciples and in us. When they asked if the blind man was affected as a result of his sin or that of his parents, the Lord Jesus instructed us. As recorded in John's gospel, "As he walked along, he saw a man blind from birth. His disciples asked him, 'Rabbi, who sinned, this man or his parents, that he was born blind?' Jesus answered, "Neither this man nor his parents sinned; he was born blind so that God's works might be revealed in him" (John 9:1–3). Through the work of pastoral care ministry, God's works are realized through us and through those to whom we minister. The causes of illness may be seen alternatively then as the Lord's testing, his stretching us in order to facilitate our spiritual growth, his strengthening us, or his developing in us a stronger reliance on him. Some even see illness and difficulties as motivators to build personal prayer and meditation resources, or as an opportunity for God to be glorified in our lives.

As with the Samaritan woman at the well in the gospel of John (4:7–42), our divine model Jesus meets us where we are and heals us as we are. We must struggle to do the same for others. The Jesus in each of us may not necessarily need to do something for someone, but we may need just to be with them; we may not be called to give but simply to offer; the need may be not for us to speak but simply to listen. We may not be able to speak peace to the wind and the waves, but we can certainly remain in the boat with those who are suffering.

The second striking issue shared among the denominations is the importance of the pastor as role model to the congregation in pastoral care issues. Not only does the pastor teach, but she must also model pastoral care. This care extends equally to all regardless of status or influence outside or inside the church. Ministers from different faith traditions share a concern that pastors represent the entire community as advocate. The ministers see health care advocacy as a justice issue of major concern.

The African American church, then, has traditionally concerned itself and must continue to concern itself with the health of the total community and the increasingly complex combinations of factors that bear on the individual's total health and ultimately on the health of the family and the community. The deacons and deaconesses visit the sick; members of the missionary society assume responsibility for ministering to the physical needs of the church community. Church members with no formal medical training conduct visitations in which prayer and encouragement are the main purposes and features. Formal analysis, or observation of the less readily discernable subtleties in a patient's condition, is left to the medical professional.

Recent changes, however, have made a new type of pastoral care visitation an absolute necessity. It is now necessary for those who plan and implement pastoral visitors' ministries to understand the social and political environment of those they serve. It is also important that those who make the visits be prepared with new skills to discern the spiritual and simple medical needs of those who are ill. Those charged with responsibility for administering the visitation program must be trained to address health care concerns in a difficult social environment. The work of pastoral care ministry has revitalized the deacons and deaconesses and brought new meaning and power to their worship in their home visits. A new effort to be attentive to the specific needs of those being visited has developed, and a new level of awareness, empathy, and grace may be seen in these human interactions.

While the pastoral care visitation requires a degree of training and competence on the part of the visitor, it is intended that the team activities supplement, not supplant, the activities of trained medical professionals. The members of the Universal Baptist Church were well prepared to participate in such a training program for a number of reasons, including the fact that the pastor had taught and preached on the importance of service to the outcast and that the church membership has demonstrated a commitment to its responsibility throughout the church's seventy-year history.

When the training began, Universal Baptist Church leaders were completing a seven-year cycle of leadership development and training. The leadership structure of the church included the board of deacons, which is traditionally responsible for conducting such visits. Missionaries and nurses also participated. The success of the training with these groups can be attributed to a visitation program based on sound biblical principles and relationships drawn between scripture and practice. The importance of the training and the consistency of the program's tenets with biblical truths were validated through the pastor's participation in the training and the response of the participants to the training.

The participants responded well when workshop leaders began sessions with prayer. Prayer and biblical authority are, for this congregation, critical and essential aspects of any training program. Participants were also attentive to uses of scripture and parables in the training sessions; evaluations reinforced the participants' concern for biblical authority behind each component of the program. The success of the program quite literally rested on the presenters' use of scriptures that show Jesus as a healer. Sincere and competent use of the Bible by presenters also established their validity in this community of believers. A failure by presenters to demonstrate an understanding and familiarity with scripture could have resulted in the failure of the training program.

Implementation: Critical Issues

The discussion and implementation of this program at the Universal Baptist Church raised many critical issues among members of the congregation, and a review of these issues may help other congregations in their efforts to initiate similar programs. One might justifiably ask how it could be possible for those who live difficult lives, surrounded by suffering, to minister to those who are in need. Members of this church community do not live in another town or another country. Many are the primary victims of the same chaos experienced by those to whom they minister, yet they have accepted the challenge. The people in this congregation have no other social or cultural framework to which they can refer when the challenges become unbearable. Service at this level is neither academic nor some exercise designed to assuage some hidden collective guilt. It is not the outgrowth of what Robert Coles calls "lofty political or social impulses, the demonstration of stoic endurance or a boost to success." Service at this level is at once a statement of collective concern for the body and a very practical impatience with the pervasive assault on human dignity. This is the service of the victimized to the victimized, accomplished by the grace of God and, therefore, infinitely transformative.

We Are All Wounded Healers

The success of the pastoral care ministry and the willingness of team members to persist have grown from a biblical mandate. The biblical teaching on service in Matthew 25:35–36 is an example of such a mandate. It is important that the pastor and the Sunday church school teachers provide regular instruction on the importance of Christian service. This issue becomes increasingly important as traditional health care services diminish, as the task of obtaining health care becomes more difficult and rule-bound, and as our population ages. Consistent teaching on the importance of service may make the retention of volunteers less difficult. As one might expect, this has been a continuing problem in the development of this pastoral visitation ministry.

Integration into Existing Ministries

Training is wonderful, but there are practical challenges to implementing a new program in a local congregation. Those who have always been responsible for making visits have to be encouraged to see the need for more specialized interventions and to recognize that they do not possess that specialized level of skill. This new area of collaboration requires sensitive relationship building and a considerable degree of trust. The older deacon whose authority in the area of home visitations has rarely been questioned might find it difficult to defer to a younger, formally trained woman in determining the needs of a chronically ill member.

Turf issues can be expected to surface when a new program design is implemented, especially where apparently similar programs exist. In order to avoid such issues, our pastor invited members of the diaconate and several visitation ministries to participate in the initial pastoral care ministry eight-week training program. Each participant was then responsible for presenting the information to other members of her or his ministry group. This technique allowed for a less difficult implementation of the program and encouraged the cooperation of members of each group.

Existing structures were modified to accommodate the goals of the pastoral ministry program. Each group of five that comprised a visitation team included a member of each of the various ministry groups. Deacons and deaconesses, according to their accustomed responsibilities for visiting the sick, made initial visits. If they saw a cause for concern, a request was made of the team, including a social worker, to make an additional visit.

Follow-through and Coordination

Program administration requires a procedure for obtaining information about those who are facing hospitalization, those already hospitalized, and those who have completed their hospital stay. Visitation request sheets are inserted into the weekly church bulletin and are taken up with the morning collection. The program administrator gathers the sheets and phone contact is made with the individual or a family member. Arrangements are made to have two members of the visitation team make an initial visit. Should issues of concern be apparent, a request is made for the team social worker to visit. Appropriate interventions then follow.

Some members of the church community appeared unaware of the existence of hospital discharge plans. Certainly, fear and concern are expected reactions in the face of a proposed hospital stay and attention to many details may be overlooked. The discharge plan appeared to be one of those details. Efforts are under way to heighten church members' awareness of the importance of advance planning when possible. In the event that planning is not possible, the social worker team member is expected to assist in this area.

Safety Concerns

The physical safety of the members of the team is of grave importance. The team must follow guidelines modeled after those followed by visiting and public health nurse programs. Before a team makes a visit, they notify the coordinator. The coordinator is the clearinghouse for all calls, referrals, and requests about those in the community who are grieving or ill. Team members carry cell phones, and one contact person is assigned to remain accessible by phone throughout the duration of the team visit.

Ongoing Supervision and Training

A continuing need exists for ongoing supervision and training and opportunities to evaluate the efficacy of team efforts. The team members must come together regularly for supervision and to process what they've learned during the visits. Pastoral visitation is not only an exercise in faith; it requires the acquisition and application of practical knowledge. It also requires that our own personal and emotional involvement be monitored as well. The involvement of a health care professional is essential if the congregation is to support the ongoing efforts of the pastoral care team.

Professional Skills

Although the program is intended to provide skills training and awareness-raising for non-professionals, the involvement of church members who work in the health profession has improved the effectiveness of the local pastoral visitation effort. Not only do those who are being served benefit, but the entire effort is enhanced by the professional relationships and links made with the wider health care community.

A pastoral visitors' training program must be designed to address far more than the physical needs of the people being served. Pastoral care instructors need to be as skilled in faith reflection and spiritual direction as they are in their various professional areas. The visitors and the instructors are transformed in the process. There has been some evidence that intentional faith reflection may contribute to the ability of volunteers to process deep questions of faith, many of which surface when people are challenged by illness and suffering. My congregation has entered such a faith journey in our efforts to grow as the Lord's servants.

The pastoral visitors' training program was extremely successful at the Universal Baptist Church. Evaluation sheets were distributed after each session, and participants indicated a high level of satisfaction with the information shared by the presenters and with the quality of the presentations. The greatest impact, however, appeared to occur at the inter- and intra-personal level. The strong truck driver cried during an exercise in which he was asked to imagine the conditions of another participant's life. He had never been asked to do this before. An opinionated, self-directed young woman realized that she had never allowed herself to just listen, in silence, for another person's pain. A deaconess shared a personal testimony about a life-changing event that she had never before felt safe enough to tell. These people were experienced in making church related visits but had never understood the importance of simply being present with one who is suffering. In spite of having made countless visits, they had never critically evaluated the specific health conditions or needs of the person being visited. The participants learned lessons impossible to fully convey.

Other changes also occurred. Participants gained a level of self-efficacy that had not been in evidence before the training occurred, and the members' response to the needs of others was heightened. There were noticeable changes in behavior among those who participated in the pastoral visitation training. Additional ministries have resulted; team members have extended their efforts into the community, inviting the participation of those in the neighborhood regardless of church affiliation. Participants in the church's effort were inspired to serve as Jesus served and to see the other person's need just as Jesus was able to see. In Mark's gospel, the Lord Jesus *saw* Levi sitting at the tax booth; the Master didn't just see the man Levi, but he saw Levi's need and entered into relationship with Levi (Mark 2:14). He entered into the space where Levi had been suffering alone and he remained with him there. As Christians, this is our tradition. By God's grace, the tradition will continue.

The implementation of a new program requires time and effort. There are innumerable "people issues" that must be worked through. New situations are sometimes difficult, even in church families! In our community, new procedures had to be established; ongoing training and supervision still need to be worked through. However, the members of the team seem committed to this ministry. We are determined to invest the prayer, time, and energy required to make the pastoral visitation ministry an effort in which the entire community experiences the Master's love and concern.

The power of the faith community must be applied to the most difficult problems and to the most difficult situations. We may lament, but on the other side of the Sea of Despair waits the victory hymn. Pharaoh may be at our backs, and we may be hemmed in on every side, *but God!* The Divine Presence gives us the power and influence and courage to stand in the face of oppression, no matter how desperate our situations appear to be. Our Savior has always specialized in extreme and seemingly hopeless situations.

For Further Reading

Coles, Robert (1993). *The Call of Service: A Witness to Idealism.* Boston: Houghton Mifflin.

Flateau, John, ed. (1998). *Brooklyn's Bridge to the Future: Strategic Plan for the Brooklyn Empowerment Zone.* Brooklyn, N.Y.: Office of Brooklyn Borough President.

Lehman, Paula D. (1998). *Faith Reflection: A Methodology for the Spiritual Emergence of Volunteers.* Dissertation, United Theological Seminary.

The New Oxford Annotated Bible: New Revised Standard Version (1989). New York: Oxford University Press.

Taylor, Mark V. C. (1999). "What Can We Say to These Things? James Melvin Washington and Preaching in the African American Church Tradition." In Dixie, Quinton Hosford, & West, Cornel, eds., *The Courage to Hope: From Black Suffering to Human Redemption,* 134–146. Boston: Beacon Press.

COMPONENTS OF
THE PARTNERS IN HEALING
IMPLEMENTATION EFFORT

❑ Educate the congregation—prepare them to accept the new pastoral visitation paradigm

❑ Brainstorm ways of integrating the new concept and practice into existing structures

❑ Select volunteers from among the congregation and include leaders from other service groups in the church

❑ Involve volunteers in developing site-specific and culture-specific aspects of the pastoral visitation ministry program

❑ Make a formal presentation of the ministry to the entire community

❑ Prepare a referral and notification system to manage visitation requests and to keep current with needs

❑ Mentor volunteers throughout the first several months of service. Supervision is essential in a group context

❑ Send them out "two by two"

❑ Provide monthly supervision/evaluation throughout the first year

❑ Develop a resource/policy manual in cooperation with supervisor

❑ Hold weekly meetings of Partners in Healing teams to work through design and implementation problems

❑ Arrange for ongoing recruitment and training of new team members

❑ Provide for ongoing presentations and updates to the congregation

❑ Involve the pastor

CONTRIBUTORS TO THIS VOLUME

Elizabeth A. Baker, D. Min., is a supervisor and instructor in the Pastoral Psychotherapy Program at the Blanton Peale Institute, New York City. She has been a guest lecturer at Fordham University and worked as a pastoral psychotherapist at Union Theological Seminary and New York's Riverside Church. She was the director of the Stamford Counseling Center in Stamford, Conn., and has a private practice in New York City.

John R. Bickle resides in Philadelphia and serves as a consultant for health care institutions interested in improving the delivery of spiritual care services. He holds a Master of Science degree in Health Administration from St. Joseph's University, Philadelphia, and has a Master of Divinity degree from St. Anthony-on-Hudson School of Theology. He is a founding member of Partners in Healing.

Kathleen M. Duffy is a laywoman currently working as a hospital chaplain. Her background includes nursing, spiritual direction, and parish ministry. She coordinates a Partners in Healing ministry at St. Francis Xavier parish in New York City.

Sarah L. Fogg is Director of Pastoral Care at Lawrence Hospital in Bronxville, N.Y. She holds a Ph.D. from Indiana University and an M.Div. from Union Theological Seminary. She is a board-certified chaplain and an ordained American Baptist Minister. She lectures frequently on pregnancy loss, visiting the sick, and family emotional process.

Curtis W. Hart is an Episcopal priest and Director of Pastoral Care and Education at the New York–Presbyterian Hospital, New York Weill Cornell Center. At Weill Medical College, Cornell University, he holds an appointment as lecturer in the Department of Medicine. He is a board-certified chaplain in the Association of Professional Chaplains and a Diplomat in Pastoral Supervision in the College of

Pastoral Supervision and Psychotherapy. He is a founding member of Partners in Healing.

Beverly Anne Musgrave, Ph.D., received her doctorate in psychology from Fielding Institute. She is an assistant professor and Co-Director of Pastoral Counseling and Spiritual Care at the Graduate School of Religion and Religious Education of Fordham University in New York City. She is the founder of Partners in Healing and has a private practice in pastoral psychotherapy.

Jacqueline C. Perez, D.O., is an attending physician at the Saint Vincent's Catholic Medical Center of New York. Through her work in the Community Medicine Department, she has explored the doctor-patient relationship in a variety of clinical settings. She is a member of the Board of Directors for Partners in Healing, Inc.

Elizabeth M. Renyi holds an M.S. degree from the Graduate School of Religion and Religious Education, Fordham University. She has served as chair of the Board of Directors for Partners in Healing and is past program director of Oasis, Inc., of Paterson, N.J. She is married and the mother of three children.

Patricia Cusack is a Dominican Sister of Mary of the Springs, Columbus, Ohio, and is currently Director of Volunteer Services at St. Vincent's Hospital in New York. She holds a doctorate degree in Adult Education from Columbia University Teachers College.

Michelle D. White, Ph.D., is a member of the ministerial staff of Universal Baptist Church in the Bedford Stuyvesant neighborhood of Brooklyn, New York. She is a graduate of the Blanton Peale Graduate Institute in New York City, received an M.Div. from Union Theological Seminary, and holds an M.S. and Ph.D. in education from Fordham University.